PRAISE FOR FROZEN ASSETS

"*Frozen Assets* will prove to be the hands-down authority on once-a-month cooking." Susan R. Sands, Publisher, *Home Words Magazine*

"This book offers relief to those tired of eating restaurant fare or expensive, over packaged convenience foods at the end of a hard day. Recommended..." *Library Journal*

"...contains recipe ideas, plus detailed instructions on how to get the maximum value from your food dollar, while also slashing meal preparation times. If you are into efficiency and want a guide to reorganizing your culinary life, this book is a must-have." Amazon.com

"Finally, a realistic way to combine the cost-effectiveness of cooking from scratch with the convenience of quick and easy meals!" Mary Hunt, Editor & Publisher, *Cheapskate Monthly Newsletter*

"This cookbook is a necessity for anyone trying to save time and money while still providing a nutritious home-cooked meal." *Home Cooking Magazine*

"This title is bound to be a favorite...because of its comprehensive scope and easy going style." *Christian Parenting Today*

"Hate to cook? Love to cook but don't have the time? Want to have more free time on a daily basis? Then this is your book. These are easy and affordable recipes, kid-tested and family-approved. Eat well and have more time—what a combination!" *Marriage Magazine*

"...provides shopping lists and delicious recipes that will help you save time in the kitchen and money in the grocery store." *The Oak Ridger*, Tennessee

"Taylor-Hough's recipes are easy, with a minimum amount of ingredients and labor. And she presents the plan with an eye toward flexibility, allowing cooks to adapt the freeze-ahead plan to their own palates and checkbooks." *Johnson City Press*

"...offers kid-tested recipes that are easy and affordable." *The Oregonian*

"After reading *Frozen Assets*, I no longer waste money buying convenience frozen foods at the grocery store. And with Deborah Taylor-Hough's method of cooking, I also save time. I highly recommend it to anyone who wants to save time and money!" Penny E. Stone, author of *365 Quick, Easy and Inexpensive Dinner Menus*

"...cooks looking to save time without resorting to expensive convenience food will find this book helpful." *Herald-Journal*

"...[this] book outlines a step-by-step plan to one dedicated day in the kitchen that will provide breakfasts, lunches and dinners for the following month." *Detroit News*

"...a cookbook well worth a second look." *The Pilot*, North Carolina

"...just about everyone will find the planning and organizational tips valuable..." *The Light Connection*

"This book belongs in every family's kitchen! One of the best time and money-savers a busy family can have." <u>Gary Foreman, Editor,</u> *The Dollar Stretcher*

"There are shopping lists and recipes for two-week and 30-day meal plans. There's even a 10-day plan designed to eliminate cooking over the Christmas and New Year holidays. What a stress reliever!" *The Daily News,* <u>Washington</u>

"Finally a book that is so cooking-friendly ANYONE can follow the steps." <u>Sherry Stacy, Weekly Radio Host, *Recipes for Life* on KVSN</u>

"Whether you cook for one month or one week, I am sure everyone can reap benefit from this book." <u>Keith C. Heirdorn, Publisher,</u> *Living Gently Quarterly*

"*Frozen Assets* will be at the top of my recommended books list!"<u>Rebecca Stuck, Advice Columnist, *Ask Miss Frugal*</u>

"And she's done an impressive job with this book, which outlines step-by-step the shopping, cooking and freezing processes that have worked so well..." <u>*Copley News Service*</u>

"...details a plan for cooking and freezing in quantity, with grocery lists, shopping lists, storage tips and dollar-stretching hints. The recipes are simple and straightforward, using everyday ingredients." <u>*Atlanta Journal*</u>

"A perfect gift for a busy homemaker." <u>*The News-Herald Newspapers*</u>

"...the book is a one-stop resource for those looking to increase their time at the family table and decrease time spent in the kitchen and drive-through lanes." *The Cookbook Collectors' Exchange*

"Frozen Assets has opened my eyes to even greater time and money savings." Steven M. Garrett, M.S., R.D., Food Security and Nutrition Education, Washington State University

"A cookbook is typically a collection of recipes. *Frozen Assets* is so much more than that. It is a very comprehensive guide to bulk freezer cooking, covering everything you need to know in great detail..." Lynn Nelson, Busy Cooks, About.Com

FROZEN ASSETS

Also by Deborah Taylor-Hough

A Simple Choice:

a practical guide for saving
your time, money and sanity

Frozen Assets Lite & Easy:

Mix and Match Recipes

Curriculum Yellow Pages (co-author)

FROZEN ASSETS

how to cook
for a day
and eat
for a month

by deborah
taylor-hough

CHAMPION PRESS, LTD.
MILWAUKEE, WISCONSIN

Library of Congress Catalog Card Number 98-072249

Cataloging-in-Publication Data
Taylor-Hough, Deborah.
  Frozen assets : how to cook for a day and eat for a
month / Deborah Taylor -Hough. —1st ed.
  p. cm.
  Includes index.
  Preassigned LCCN: 98-72249
  ISBN: 1-891400-61-4

  1. Make-ahead cookery 2. Frozen foods. 3. Quantity
cooking. I. Title.

  TX610.T39 1998
      641.5'55
      QBI98-834

Manufactured in Canada
10 9 8 7 6

Book Design by Pilot Publishing, Milwaukee, Wisconsin

DEDICATION

This book is dedicated to Stuart, Kelsey, Ian and Shannon who put up with endless new recipes and freezer experiments. You, my loving family, provided never-tiring support and encouragement; and also allowed me the time to write, study, maintain web-pages, answer E-mail and cook.

Thank you!

ACKNOWLEDGMENTS

My deepest appreciation to:

Dad ~ You gave me the computer which ultimately led to writing this book. How can I thank you enough?

Brook N. ~ You believed in this project as much as I did. Thanks for your encouragement and editing.

Vicki M. ~ Thanks for suggesting a freezer-meal discussion and planting the seeds in my mind for this book.

Di J. and Chris S. ~ Your neighborliness (and the use of your large stockpots!) made much of this possible.

· Lisa M., Evelyn S., Karen S., Catherine L. and Barb M. ~ Your friendship, prayers and faith in me never wavered.

Leon F. ~ You always had a moment to share your experience and practical knowledge with a new writer.

Steven G. ~ From your example, I learned to run an effective E-mail discussion group.

Deb V., Gloriamarie A., Lynn N. and Sue (in Scotland) ~ Your cooking wisdom, recipes, advice, and humor never failed to inspire me.

And to all the other participants on the OAMC discussion group, thank you for sending your tips, questions, comments, recipes, encouragement and most of all, your friendship—without all of you, this book never would've been written. I wish I could mention each of you by name, but there's not enough room on this page for the hundreds of personal acknowledgments it would require. (But I know who you are, and I appreciate every one of you!)

TABLE OF CONTENTS

Chapter Seven

Chapter Eight

Chapter Nine

Holiday Breakfast Casserole - McBreakfast - Breakfast Burritos -
Mix-n-Match Quick Bread - Mix-n-Match Soup - Debi's Million Dollar
Chocolate Chip Cookies - Multi-Purpose Baking Mix - Pancakes -
Waffles - Biscuits - Shortcake - Snack Cake - Dumplings - Pizza Crust

Chapter Ten

APPENDICES

Index and Worksheets

INTRODUCTION

I've been using bulk cooking methods for five years. The book, *Once-a-Month Cooking*, by Mimi Wilson and Mary Beth Lagerborg, revolutionized the way I feed my family. Although I found the recipes in *Once-a-Month Cooking* more expensive than my budget allowed, I adapted many of their techniques using my own recipes, and we've been saving money on groceries ever since. Also, not cooking a main dish from scratch every day allows me to save both time and effort. (My time is worth money, too!)

In February of 1997, an e-mail discussion began between Vicki Madden and myself on the subject of cooking for the freezer. Vicki had visited my frugal living web page and noticed that I enjoyed freezer-meal cooking. She had recently prepared a special Christmas gift for her boyfriend, a freezer full of frozen dinners. Vicki dropped me a note and asked if I'd like to share thoughts and experiences about freezer-meal cooking. Soon we were exchanging tips, ideas and favorite recipes. At the time I was a stay-at-home mother of three and Vicki was a single working mother of one; the input from our divergent lifestyles and family sizes made for a fun and stimulating conversation.

On a whim, I asked other online friends if they'd be interested in joining our once-a-month cooking (OAMC) discussion. I was surprised when nearly everyone I contacted replied, "Yes! I'd love to join a group like that!" Thus began the idea with a mind of its own. Our little two person conversation grew to include hundreds of people from all walks of life, family backgrounds, economic levels and geographical locations. I now maintain a popular OAMC web page which averages 4,000+ visitors each month—this is obviously an idea with wide appeal.

Many of the tips, recipes and comments throughout this cookbook come from the international group of men and women who have participated in my online, OAMC mailing list. This book has been written in response to the demand I've received for an affordable and easy-to-follow book on freezer meals for people that are new to the concept.

My desire is that this book will help fill that need.

~Debi

1

The Attraction of Frozen Assets

Following the premature birth of our first child, a group of friends from church filled our freezer with over two weeks of frozen meals. Between frequent visits to the hospital nursery and the normal stresses of starting a new family, those meals in the freezer were a lifesaver.

During a later pregnancy, I wound up on bed rest for nearly four weeks. Once again, the ladies from church came to our aid with frozen dinners. One woman overwhelmed me when she showed up at my door laden with several shopping bags full of ready-to-cook frozen dinners—all from her personal stock of freezer meals.

The meals brought after my daughter's premature birth were my introduction to the concept of frozen meals. Since then, I've applied this method to our regular family menus and have saved substantial time, effort and money in the process. Some cookbooks refer to this as investment cooking, once-a-month cooking, bulk cooking or cooking ahead. I call my method Frozen Assets, since dinner in the freezer can be like money in the bank.

Whether you're a stay-at-home mom creatively trying to make ends meet; a working parent searching for more hours in your hectic day; a single person looking for ideas for preparing homecooked meals without leftovers; someone interested in the outreach opportunities frozen meals can provide; or anyone who needs to save money or find a few more hours in their day; Frozen Assets could be your answer.

The people I've met who are actively involved with freezer-meal cooking methods represent a large and growing cross-section of the population: single, married, stay-at-home parents, part-time workers, full-time working parents, working couples with no children, business owners, big happy families and small happy families. And they're living all over the world—throughout the United States, Canada, the United Kingdom, New Zealand, Australia and elsewhere.

Freezer-meal cooks are also active in a variety of personal pursuits which put frequent demands on their time and financial resources: full-time careers, consulting work, freelance writing, genealogy, volunteering, PTA, transporting children to various functions, sports, homeschooling, Sunday School teachers, leading and attending various types of study groups, co-ops, military functions, church activities, community events, piano recitals, music ministry, knitting, adult education, college studies and more.

People from all walks of life are reaping the benefits of this simple, common sense approach to cooking and meal planning.

In a recent survey I asked the question, "What first attracted you to make-ahead cooking?" The answers I received from the survey participants were varied. Maybe you can relate to some of the following statements:

"I hate coming home and trying to figure out what to have for dinner, especially because I don't enjoy cooking. I can put up with it for one day—if it means I don't have to cook for the rest of the month."

"I was attracted by the idea of saving money—not having to buy fast food because I'm too busy to think about cooking every night even though I love to cook."

"Trying to make ends meet with this tribe is a constant challenge and I can use all the help I can get!"

"I like the idea of the organization presented in OAMC. It seems that it would help out the budget as well."

"I am diabetic. I also love to eat out due to being too tired to cook. I thought if I already had healthy food prepared I'd be more apt to stick to my diabetic routine and not spend so much money at restaurants."

"My mother recently passed away and I'm worried about my dad not eating properly. I'm going to freeze single servings of our regular family meals to put in Dad's freezer. That way I can be assured he's eating a hot, home-cooked meal each evening instead of just another TV dinner."

"I'm currently trying to cut corners wherever possible in order to get our financial house in order—cooking for the freezer sounds like it's definitely a time-saver and money-saver."

"I like being organized so I like to have meals in the freezer or a supper ready in the fridge for the next night we're busy."

"As a homeschooler, I have a lot more flexibility in what we can do. If we spend all day at a museum or park, all we have to do is pop dinner in the oven when we get home. It really cuts down on those grab-a-burger-on-the-way-home meals."

"We only get paid once a month. It would help our budgeting."

"Bulk buying and bulk cooking—I love it!"

"I love not having to think about what to fix for dinner each night—5:00 P.M. is a stressful time at my house—hubby is just wrapping up work and my daughter wants attention. Now I can relax and enjoy my family."

"I read that cooking for the freezer would save time and money, and enable me to have meals available if someone had a need in their family (sickness, new baby, etc.)."

"I'm single and practice a modified version of cooking once for a month. I started this when I was commuting by train—a three hour round trip plus a very stressful eight hour day. When I arrived home it was usually

bread and cheese and fall into bed, so I developed a routine of cooking ahead for the freezer."

"Invariably I would stand at the refrigerator every night at 5:00 P.M. wondering, 'What am I going to fix?' After 12 to 15 hours at work each day, I didn't want to even think about cooking. I also wanted to save money by not eating out as often."

"The time and money savings, as well as the added convenience of not worrying about what the kids were going to eat when I was at work, attracted me to freezer meals."

Although the reasons for bulk cooking are varied, the basic premise remains the same—saving time, effort and money by creating a stock of homemade meals in your freezer for later use.

You may choose to cook all day and stock up a month's worth of meals in your freezer (or two months of meals—or more!). You might spread your bulk cooking out over the course of several days. You may decide to cook freezer meals periodically taking advantage of sales at the market. You might like doubling or tripling recipes as you cook during the week—adding the extra batches to your stash of Frozen Assets.

Whatever method of cooking for the freezer you choose, I believe you'll find Frozen Assets to be a wise, money-saving, time-saving investment in your family's health, peace of mind and financial well-being.

"Help! My Freezer Is Too Small," and other Frequently Asked Questions

The following are questions frequently asked about frozen meals and make-ahead cooking.

"I only have the small freezer above my refrigerator. Can I still do a full month worth of cooking ahead?"

You might want to consider twice-a-month cooking at first until you get used to the method, and used to packing your freezer tightly. Eventually, you may be able to store the entire month's worth of entrees in your fridge-top freezer with careful planning. Use heavy duty freezer bags to freeze food more compactly than in casserole dishes or foil pans. Freeze the bags flat and stack them carefully. Clear out non-essentials from the freezer before cooking day. Wait until the freezer clears out later in the month before stocking up on frozen bread, ice cream, etc. To save space, prepare meals with sauces to pour over noodles or rice, but don't freeze the noodles or rice ahead; cook them up fresh when you serve the sauce.

"I don't have much money to buy a new freezer but I would like to purchase a separate freezer. Where should I go to find one?"

Ask friends, relatives and neighbors to keep an eye out for people who are moving out of state or updating their kitchen. I've known several people who have gotten freezers for free just by making a few phone calls. Check the newspaper. Look at garage sales, yard sales and appliance repair stores. Try auctions of dented white goods.

"How do you keep track of which meals are in the freezer and which have been used?"

Post a list of all meals on your freezer door—either on paper or a small white board. Mark the meals off the list as you use them.

"How do I cook for an entire day with two toddlers underfoot?"

Some possibilities: cook with a friend and then trade off childcare and cooking duty; have a spouse or relative take the children out for the day; enlist a friend or neighbor to watch your kids that day and offer to watch hers in return; let the kids spend the day with their grandparents; barter some frozen home-cooked meals in exchange for a few hours of baby-sitting.

"How do I know what will freeze well and what won't?"

If you're unsure, freeze a small amount as a test. For a listing of foods that don't freeze well or that change in the freezing process, see Appendix A.

"What can I use for freezer containers?"

Plastic food storage boxes, metal, glass and ceramic bakeware work well. Be sure to check garage sales and thrift stores for these items. Freezer bags also work well. Use heavy-duty bags specifically intended for freezer usage—not just the regular food storage bags.

If you prepare and store freezer meals in rectangular shapes, you may actually get more into your freezer than before since you won't have lumpy packages and round containers taking up excess room.

Almost any plastic food-grade container is safe for freezing food, but don't use plastic containers in the microwave unless they say they're safe for that purpose. Plastics not specifically made for heating can seep harmful chemicals into your food.

You can also line baking pans with heavy-duty aluminum foil. Add your meal; cook if necessary; let cool. Put the baking pan filled with the meal into the freezer. When the meal is frozen solid, remove the frozen meal and foil from baking dish; wrap meal completely with more foil; label and freeze. To reheat, simply place the frozen foil-wrapped meal back into the original pan you used for freezing.

"If I do the complete thirty-day-meal cooking, will it cost a lot for the initial investment in a full month's worth of food?"

It depends on how elaborate your meals are and how much you cook from scratch. Convenience foods are much more expensive than their homemade counterparts. It might cost a bit more the first time, but because you'll be purchasing some items in bulk, the cost could actually be quite a bit less than you would expect. Recipes that use a lot of pre-made items can be expensive to prepare. Chapter Ten contains a collection of money-saving ideas for grocery shopping.

"My kitchen is tiny. How can I handle a large amount of cooking in such a small space?"

Make extra counter space by turning off the gas stove and lighting burners as needed. Set up a card table in the living room. Use the kitchen or dining room table for food prep. If the washer and dryer are near the kitchen use these for additional countertops. Organize yourself by thinking through your cooking steps ahead of time.

"How do I label things? What sort of labels, pens, etc. do I need? What should I write on the labels?"

Inexpensive freezer labels applied to the foil before freezing will usually work fine. If you use freezer paper, you can write directly on it with a grease pencil. You can use a Sharpie brand permanent marker to write directly on the foil or freezer bag. A wet-erase marker also works well on foil. Avoid masking tape, since it won't stick at low temperatures. Another labeling suggestion is double-bagging meals in freezer bags and slipping an index card with the labeling information between the two bags.

On your label write: the name of the meal, date frozen, number of servings, reheating directions and any other special instructions (i.e. sprinkle with one cup grated cheese before baking, etc.).

"I love this idea of cooking for my freezer, but I don't have a full day available for cooking. Are there other ways of cooking ahead?"

You can cook three or four meals at a time rather than a whole month's worth. Or spread out your cooking by preparing all of your chicken recipes one day, ground beef recipes another, spaghetti sauce recipes on a different day, and then vegetarian or cooked bean recipes on an additional day. Doubling and tripling recipes will also help you quickly build up a stock of frozen meals. It really doesn't take more time to make a large pot of spaghetti for freezing extras than it does to make a single meal's worth of sauce.

"Are all the freezer meals casseroles and pasta with sauce dishes?"

You can freeze almost anything: soups, casseroles, sandwiches, meals to serve over rice, chicken dishes, etc.

"I'm a vegetarian. Any special tips?"

There shouldn't be any problem adapting this method to vegetarian menus. When you prepare your regular recipes try freezing a single portion before you attempt a large batch of freezer meals. (This tip applies to any recipe you haven't tried in the freezer.) Tofu, TVP (texturized vegetable protein) and cooked dry beans all freeze well.

"Are there special pots and pans, utensils or appliances I should consider having on hand to make the big cooking day go easier?"

~ A food processor is helpful for chopping large quantities of onions, celery, etc.

~ Good, sharp knives.

~ Several large stock pots (the heavier, the better).

~ Long handled spoons for stirring and mixing.

~ A good can opener (an electric one isn't necessary but will make the process easier).

~ Crockpots are helpful.

~ If you have a Salad Shooter, it works well for grating large amounts of cheese.

~ An automatic bag-sealing machine does a great job sucking the air out of bags and sealing them for the freezer. These can often be found inexpensively at garage sales.

~ If you're cooking breakfast items ahead, buy or borrow a waffle iron to make homemade frozen waffles (these are much tastier than the ones bought from the grocery freezer case).

note: You don't necessarily have to run out and purchase all of these items right away. I often borrow a neighbor's large stock pot and waffle iron on my cooking days.

3

A Day In The Life of Frozen Assets

The following is a description of a bulk cooking session at my house. Many people have told me it proved helpful while planning their first round of freezer meals.

Thursday - Early Evening

I've stared at my empty freezer long enough.

Tonight I'll sit down, plan my month's menus and make out a shopping list for tomorrow morning. Saturday will be cooking day. It takes me about six hours of one day to complete a full month of cooking main dinner meals. A long day of cooking, true, but having a homecooked meal available every day for a month with no more fuss than just the preparation of a side dish and salad, is heaven! One of the best parts of cooking ahead is taking those armloads of yummy dinners out to the freezer.

My husband's work schedule is one of the main reasons I tried OAMC in the first place. I knew I needed to do something differently to work around our unusual family schedule. My husband often works odd shifts so we frequently need to eat our main meal at noon during the week. If I don't have dinner in the freezer, I end up spending much of the morning (our family time) preparing our noon meal. Or we run out to the local taco stand for $0.59 tacos.

A friend suggested cooking for the freezer so I wouldn't have to take up our only time together as a family with cooking and meal preparation. My initial response was, "I'd love to try that, but we don't have a separate freezer—just the little one over the refrigerator. I don't have enough room to store a month's worth of meals."

My friend encouraged me to start small, doing twice-a-month cooking and packing the meals in freezer bags for more compact stacking in the freezer. It sounded reasonable. I rolled up my sleeves and gave twice-a-month cooking a try. Those two weeks of frozen meals were wonderful.

Eventually I learned by using freezer bags, I could pack an entire month's worth of cooking in our little fridge-top freezer. The first two weeks of the month we didn't have room for frozen bread or ice cream, but having those prepared meals was definitely more important to my sanity than stocking up on bread and eating frozen desserts the entire month.

Recently my father purchased a larger freezer for himself and gave his small chest freezer to us. (Thanks, Dad!) Now I don't have to freeze every dinner in a freezer bag and we can stock up on bread from the bakery thrift stores again. With the separate freezer, I even find ice cream in the house now and then.

I want to encourage those of you who are thinking, "Someday I'll try once-a-month cooking, *after* I get a bigger freezer," give it a go, anyway. Try twice-a-month cooking stored in freezer bags to start.

I've discovered that buying in bulk for these big cooking days can easily save enough money to pay for a good used freezer. Check your newspaper ads. You never know what kind of deals you might come across. Ask friends, relatives and neighbors to let you know if they hear of anyone moving out of state or remodeling their kitchen. I've known several families who have gotten freezers for free, just by making a few phone calls. You never know what you might come across when you start asking around.

I need to sit down with my paper, pen and favorite cookbooks. Planning night tonight. . . for tomorrow I shop!

Thursday Night - Later

The first part of my OAMC is done—menu planning. This is what I'm going to make:

Sloppy Joes (3 meals)

Broccoli Quiche (3 meals)

Spaghetti (3 meals)

Chicken Creole (3 meals)

French Bread Pizza (2 meals)

Enchiladas (5 meals)

Cabbage Casserole (5 meals)

Veggie-Fish Dinner (4 meals)

Broccoli Chicken (4 meals)

Baked Macaroni Casserole (4 meals)

Scalloped Potatoes with Ham (5 meals)

That list means 41 meals will be stacked in my freezer by Saturday night. There will also be at least four meals of homemade vegetable chicken soup made from leftovers thrown into the chicken stock.

My personal freezer meals cookbook is a simple three-ring binder. I've filled it with plastic page protectors that I slip recipes into, shopping lists and other freezer-meal related information. I'm always updating my notebook as I find new recipes and tips.

I have several meal plans that I often follow, but I adapt the plan to what I have on hand, or any specific requests that my family makes. A while ago, I set up master shopping lists for my favorite meal plans. I ran off a supply of photocopies and I keep the shopping lists in the opening pages of my notebook. When it's time to plan my menu and go shopping, I can slip one of the master shopping lists out of its page protector and I'm ready to add to the list as needed. (This saves having to re-think my entire shopping list each time.)

The next page in my notebook is a list called "Order of Preparation of 30 Meals." I have everything pretty well laid out: what I need to cook the night before; what I need to do first; what order to prepare the meals; etc. I have the recipes I use most frequently in the next section of my notebook. I have a separate section for other recipes that have already been adapted to my way of freezer meal cooking, and then another section of frequently used recipes my family loves. I'll try to incorporate more of those recipes into my OAMC plans.

Eventually, I hope to have six different master lists so I would only have to repeat the same monthly plan twice a year.

Tomorrow I shop. I'll let you have a look at my shopping list and the final bill after I'm done.

Friday Afternoon

My shopping trip took just over one hour (about 70 minutes including check out time). I do all my grocery shopping at one store since I'm always strapped for time when I shop. With only one car, my time at the store is limited. I could probably save money if I shopped around for better prices at different stores, but my time and effort is worth money, too. The store I've chosen for my regular shopping is the one I've found to be generally cheaper all around than the other stores in town.

To purchase ingredients for 40+ main dish meals to feed our family of five (plus salad fixings, fruits, vegetables, shampoo, dish soap, paper products, milk, eggs, cereal, peanut butter, jelly, bread, etc.) I spent $166 grocery shopping on Friday. I had taken $180 with me to the store so after everything was said and done, I had enough money left to buy myself an espresso and a U-Bake Pizza (large pepperoni for $5.99) for our dinner on shopping day. Nice treat.

People have asked what exactly I was able to purchase for so little money. Some of the items on my master shopping list I already had on hand, but I also needed to stock up on a few things I normally have around—so I guess it all balances out.

Several weeks ago, one of our local grocery stores had a sale on ground beef (10 pound packages for $0.99 per pound) so I had already purchased my ground beef, divided it into one pound packages, and put it into the freezer. We also had enough ham in the freezer for the Scalloped Potatoes with Ham recipe. To save money when I buy ham, I almost always purchase turkey ham—especially if it's going to be added into a recipe and not eaten alone. Someone had given me 12 one-pound cans of tomato sauce, so I didn't need to buy that item, either. I also had quite a bit of frozen and canned vegetables around, so I didn't need to purchase any additional vegetables for side dishes. I'll have to restock in two weeks when my husband gets paid again, though.

If I had purchased the above mentioned items, it would've added $10 for the ground beef, $3 for the turkey ham, $2 for the tomato sauce, and about $5 for the frozen vegetables. Adding that to the $166 I spent on Friday, my total bill would've been about $186.

Here's what I purchased:

2 pounds of white fish (whatever was on sale)

2 whole chickens

2 pounds of bulk Italian sausage

2 packages hot dogs

2 taco seasoning packets

10 pounds of onions

3 large heads cabbage

2 pounds of carrots

4 pounds of broccoli

1 bunch celery

2 large green peppers

10 pounds of potatoes

2 heads lettuce

10 pounds of oranges

5 pounds of bananas

2 small cans of tomato paste

4 cans of Italian stewed tomatoes

1 can green chilies

1 large can of sliced black olives

4 jars good quality spaghetti sauce

Soda crackers

2 cans of enchilada sauce

1 box of Licorice Spice tea

Cornmeal

Biscuit mix

Liquid foundation (make-up)

4 pounds of cheddar cheese

1 pound of mozzarella cheese

3 gallons 2% milk

1 large carton of fat-free sour cream

18 eggs

Paper napkins

Ream of computer paper

Toilet paper

Paper towels

30 corn tortillas

5 pounds of spaghetti noodles

2 pounds of macaroni noodles

1½ cups millet

Large bag of Asian rice

Olive oil

1 pound of margarine

Large bottle of lemon juice

4 loaves of sandwich bread

1 loaf of French bread (for French Bread Pizza)

3 packs of hamburger buns

2 packs of hot dog buns

12 (8-inch) square foil pans

Dish soap

Kitty litter

Cat food

1 gallon of vinegar

Large bottle of ketchup

Mustard

Worcestershire sauce

Peanut butter

Jelly

2 packages of store-brand allergy medicine

Aluminum foil

Breakfast cereal

When the cashier bagged up my groceries, there were fourteen shopping bags full. I frequently hear amazed comments from cashiers about how little my groceries cost. They tell me when they see that amount of groceries, it's usually well over $250—if not closer to $300.   There's no great secret to shopping carefully. A penny saved here and there can add up quickly when purchasing large amounts of food. (I've included a list of money-saving tips for grocery shopping in Chapter Ten).

I usually purchase store brands unless I know for certain that my family doesn't like them. For example, I've tried making my spaghetti sauce with jars of generic sauce. That got a big thumbs down from everyone. Now I purchase good quality name brand sauce or I make my own. Usually one of the big brands is on sale so I purchase the sale brand. My family can really tell the difference between cheap spaghetti sauce and the better brands. With other items, they're not quite so picky. I try generic items or store brands and if they don't go over well, I don't use them again.

Sunday Afternoon

Thursday night I did my menu planning. Friday I shopped. Saturday I cooked. And by Sunday morning I had over 40 meals in my freezer. Phew....What a relief to be done with it for another month.

We are a family of five: Dad, Mom, eleven-year-old girl, eight-year-old boy and three-year-old girl. My husband is one of those people who can eat twice as much as any other person on the planet and never gain a pound. (I am not like that, by the way. I can gain weight just looking at pictures of food in magazines.) My son can eat four full bowls of breakfast cereal in the morning and still be hungry.

Friday night I cooked the chicken in a large stockpot and put it in the refridgerator to cool overnight. I also made spaghetti sauce on Friday since it goes together so quickly (ended up with four meals of spaghetti and two for pizza), and I browned the ground beef and chopped the vegetables (onions, pepper, celery, carrots).

This was my order of preparation on cooking day (more or less):

De-bone and chop chicken. Put broth in refrigerator.
Cook rice.
Cut ham into ½ inch cubes.
Cook and slice potatoes.
Prepare meals.
Use leftover vegetables, meats, tomato sauce, noodles, etc. to make soup with the broth from cooking the chicken.

Total time spent cooking on Friday night and Saturday was about seven hours including a break for lunch and a visit from extended family members in the afternoon. The relatives who stopped by didn't know I cooked bulk freezer meals, so they were curious about what I was doing. It became educating-the-relatives day at my house. One of them stayed in the kitchen with me for about 20 minutes, watching me cook and asking questions. He's fascinated by how things work, how activities save on efficiency, productivity and that sort of thing. I think my explanations passed muster.

I realized after I was done cooking on Saturday that an added benefit of cooking ahead is that I have more desire to prepare other things during the week when I'm not so focused on getting a main dinner meal prepared each day. When I know I only have to warm something up, I tend to do more extra baking and special cooking. I enjoy cooking, but the daily-ness of it wears thin after awhile. For me, Frozen Assets restores the joy of cooking special things. Tomorrow, I'm going to fix a batch of my Million Dollar Chocolate Chip Cookies and some homemade cornbread to go with our freezer meal of enchiladas.

And that's the end of my description of a day in the life of cooking ahead at my house. I hope it was helpful and gave you some food (pardon the pun!) for thought.

4

The "Ins and Outs" of Meal Planning

Although the technique of cooking one day for an entire month's worth of meals is popular right now, there are other methods of cooking ahead that may be more user-friendly, especially for people new to the idea. I recommend starting with small, manageable steps. If the idea of once-a-month cooking is intimidating, try twice-a-month or once-a-week cooking. Same methods, but less work at one time.

Another easy and painless way to start building up a supply of Frozen Assets is doubling or tripling recipes as you prepare them during the week. If you're making a casserole for tonight's dinner—prepare three instead. This way you can eat one and freeze the other two for later meals. Tripling recipes for one week will give you a two week stock of frozen meals with very little extra effort. When you prepare a double or triple batch (one to eat and the others to freeze), set the freezer batches aside a few minutes before they're fully cooked. Slightly undercooking meats, pastas and vegetables prevents overcooking and that warmed-over flavor when reheating after freezing.

Cooking a large pot of spaghetti sauce can help establish your Frozen Assets. The last time I made spaghetti sauce I added to my freezer three meals of lasagna, two meals of pizza and four meals of sauce to serve over pasta. Nine meals from one easy cooking session—not a bad return on my investment.

Often ground beef or turkey will go on sale for a great price if purchased in bulk. I stock up on sale priced meats, cook the meals ahead and add to my Frozen Assets.

Meatballs prepared ahead can be served in a variety of ways: in homemade vegetable or minestrone soup; with condensed mushroom soup and sour cream to create a stroganoff served over rice or noodles; with brown gravy and potatoes, or rice; with barbecue or spaghetti sauce served in small French rolls for sandwiches. Meatloaf freezes well and leftovers make wonderful hot or cold sandwiches.

Andrea, the mother of a two-year-old and six months pregnant with twins, is starting her investment cooking for those busy post-partum days. Realizing her hands will soon be full (literally!), she says, "I don't have the stamina to devote an entire day to standing on my feet cooking, unless I want to send myself into labor right now! I'm going to triple recipes of easy meals every night until the babies come. I know the extra work now will pay off big when I find myself less crazy over meal preparation as I'm caring for our new little ones."

Recently divorced or widowed individuals often find themselves overwhelmed with the idea of cooking every meal for just one person. It's an incredibly stressful time of life and people need to guard their health by eating regular, healthy meals. Many people facing sudden singleness end up frequenting the local drive-thru restaurants or stocking up on TV dinners from the grocery freezer case. It's easier and healthier just to reach into the freezer each day and pull out a homecooked meal that's ready to heat and serve.

Adapting these methods for singles is a common dilemma facing many cooks who are considering cooking ahead. I've prepared a list of suggestions in Appendix C for the single person desiring the convenience of freezer meals.

Getting Started With Ease

If you're new to freezer meal cooking, I recommend starting with one of this book's suggested meal plans. This way you won't have to focus on developing a plan from scratch—just follow the simple steps that are provided. After completing this routine a couple of times you'll begin to sense the patterns which will make adapting your own recipes much easier. Read through the planning section of this book to get a feel for what you'll be doing but don't worry about remembering every detail. The menu plans will guide you step-by-step through the entire process.

Menu Choice and Planning For The Trail Blazers

So you want to start right in with your own family recipes and make your own meal plan? Great! First, we need to do a little planning. To begin with, figure out how often you and your family are willing to eat the same meal in a single month. Some people refuse to eat the same meal more than once during a four week period—others don't mind eating the same meal as often as four or five times a month (providing it's not four days in a row). If you decide to eat each meal twice during the month, you will need to choose 15 recipes. I usually choose 10 recipes and triple them for a month's worth of meals. Many of the recipes in this book have already been doubled or tripled for your convenience.

When preparing your meal plan choose foods you're certain your family will enjoy. There are few things worse for a freezer meal cook than a freezer filled with food no one will eat. The recipes you choose for a 30-day cooking experience should be simple. An experienced freezer meal cook told me, "If you can't visualize the steps in your mind, it's too complicated!"

Try to choose a variety of main dishes. For example, choose several from each category: poultry, ground beef, pork, seafood, cheese, pasta, cooked dried beans, etc.

I base my monthly plan on what's currently stored in my cupboards or freezer. I also take into account sales at the local market.

The following types of dishes work especially well for the freezer: sauces (tomato, meat, gravy), main dishes, casseroles, stews, soups, meat pies, meat dishes in gravy (Swiss steak, meatballs), cooked poultry, roasts, chops, burgers, tofu, TVP, sandwiches (omit jelly, mayonnaise and lettuce), shellfish, most baked goods (cookies, breads, cakes), goulashes, meatloaf and cooked dried beans.

The following types of meals don't work well in the freezer: egg-based sauces, milk or cream-based sauces, salads, stuffed poultry, dishes with bread crumbs or dry toppings (add toppings after freezing and before reheating), fish steaks and fillets and baked fruit pies (soggy). See Appendix A for a more complete list of cautionary freezer foods.

I recommend implementing your cooking plan over a course of three days. I like to plan one day. In the evening of day two, I usually do my shopping and prepare as much as I can ahead of time. On day three, I do the actual meal assembly which takes about six to seven hours.

Making a List and Checking it Twice (Shopping)

To simplify meal planning for the month, I take out a blank calendar page and fill in all the meals that I plan to prepare on the calendar. Writing the meals down helps to prevent accidentally serving several ground beef meals in a row, or winding up with three meals of spaghetti sauce for the last week of the month. I've often used a blank magnetic wipe-off calendar on my refrigerator, but a regular calendar page or daily planner works just as well.

The day before you shop, take a look at the recipes you've chosen. Write down every ingredient (and the exact amounts) on a sheet of paper. Then go through your cupboards and refrigerator, crossing off everything you already have on hand. Check amounts carefully. If you need three 16-ounce jars of tomato sauce (48 ounces total), make sure you actually have the correct amount in ounces on hand before crossing that item off your list. After the inventory of your cupboards, the remaining ingredients will be your shopping list.

Next, figure out what sort of containers you'll be using for freezing. If you need to purchase freezer bags, plastic wrap, foil or aluminum trays, add these items to your shopping list.

Organizing your shopping list according to categories (i.e. meat, dairy, produce, canned goods, etc.) makes shopping easier and faster. I know the layout at my grocery store, so I organize my list according to store aisles.

Some shopping tips:

~ Don't shop hungry. You might get tired and weak if you're hungry and doing a huge shopping trip, plus you'll be more susceptible to impulse buys if you're hungry in the store.

~ Buy in bulk when possible. If your recipes need four 8-ounce cans of tomato paste, look for one 24-ounce can. The cost per ounce will usually be significantly less in a larger package.

~ If you find you're doing a lot of bulk buying, you might consider contacting the manufacturer directly, saving even more money. A warehouse club may offer significant savings as well.

~ Familiarize yourself with common can sizes. Some cans look similar in size, but hold different amounts.

~ Stores often place the most expensive items at eye level. Look on the lowest and highest shelves for potential bargains.

~ Compare the cost of various forms of food—fresh, frozen, canned and dried—using cost per serving.

~ Try generic or store brands. If they meet your quality needs and are okay with your family's individual tastes, you can save money by using private brand labels.

~ Choose the grade and quality of meats or produce that best fits your intended use. Use the most inexpensive form when shape, uniformity of size and color are not important.

~ Remember that you pay for fancy labels or extra packaging. Choose foods that are simply packaged.

~ Avoid convenience foods if you're trying to save money. Homemade alternatives are usually less expensive.

~ Leave your children at home when doing your major grocery shopping so you can concentrate on prices and finish your shopping as quickly as possible.

After you've arrived home from shopping, put away all perishable foods in your refrigerator, leaving out canned goods and other items needed for cooking the next day. This will save you the hassle of putting everything away, only to take it all out again the next morning. Every little bit of time and effort you can save when bulk cooking will be appreciated.

Steps for a Successful Cooking Experience

Your first experience with a big cooking day will probably be the most difficult and longest, but you'll learn shortcuts and personal preferences as you go along. Each subsequent bulk cooking day will get easier. After the big cooking day is done, you might ask yourself, "What did I do that for?" But after about two days of eating ready-made yummy meals, you'll forget all the labor that went into that freezer full of food.

Sort Your Recipes

Separate your recipes according to main protein: chicken, ground beef, dried beans, ham, etc. Plan on preparing the recipes in groups according to main ingredients. Read through your recipes and break them down into steps. Plan to do similar steps together. If you'll need to brown ground beef for tacos, spaghetti sauce and Sloppy Joes, brown all the meat together (maybe the night before)—then divide the browned meat when preparing the recipes.

Post Your Recipes for Easy Visibility

I keep my tried-and-true freezer recipes in plastic page protectors organized by main protein type in a three ring binder. This way I can actually take the pages out of my notebook while I'm cooking and lay them on the table, tape them to the wall, or hang them by magnets on the refrigerator door.

Prepare Ahead

Prepare things ahead as much as possible. Decide which items to prepare the evening before (chop vegetables, grate cheese, prepare spaghetti sauce, boil chicken, brown ground beef, etc.). It's easier to add your chopped onions or grated cheese to your recipes if they're already prepared. A food processor is helpful at this stage of meal preparation. The evening before the big cooking day, I usually brown ground beef, boil my chickens, prepare spaghetti sauce, chop vegetables and grate cheese. Restaurants usually hire someone just to do the advance preparation, making the cooking process easier for the cooks. You might want to consider "hiring" your older children as your "prep cooks."

Preparing Chicken for Recipes

If you cook the chicken the night before, you can simply add the chicken as needed to your recipes on cooking day. To prepare, boil chicken(s) in a large Dutch oven or stock pot with enough water to fully cover the chicken. Add several stalks of celery and some sliced onion. Boil until the meat is white to the bone and falling off the bone easily. After the chicken is finished cooking, cool slightly and place the pot in refrigerator to cool completely overnight. The fat will congeal on top of the pot, so you can easily scoop it away in the morning. After you've scooped off the fat, remove the chicken from the broth and de-bone. Cut the meat into bite-sized portions and place into a large bowl. Save the broth from the cooked chicken for making soup at the end of the day.

Get Ready, Get Set!

Before you begin your big day of cooking, assemble all necessary utensils, pots, pans, measuring cups, appliances, etc. You don't want to be scrambling around your kitchen looking for measuring spoons in the midst of a month's worth of cooking.

Sink O'Soap

While cooking, keep the sink filled with warm, soapy water. This way you can wash pots, pans, measuring cups, spoons and other cooking utensils as you go. If you keep ahead of messes as you progress through the day, the cleanup won't become overwhelming.

If you don't usually wear an apron while cooking, this would be a good time to start. You also might choose to wear older clothes so your good clothes won't wind up with spills or food stains. Always keep your hands, equipment and work areas clean to prevent contamination. Wash hands frequently, especially after handling raw meats. Tie back long hair.

Go For It! - Three Easy Tips

TIP ONE: Chop vegetables and grate cheese first thing on cooking day if you didn't chop them the day before.

TIP TWO: Prepare your most complicated recipes early in the day while you're still fresh.

TIP THREE: Pack foods in quantities that will be used for a single family-sized meal.

Keeping the "Fresh" in Your "Frozen"

To prevent overcooking, or that warmed-over taste, slightly undercook foods that will be reheated after freezing. Cook vegetables and meats until just tender, not soft. Undercook pasta and rice (for best results use converted rice).

When Your Stamina is Simmering

Physical exhaustion is a common complaint after a full day of cooking. These tips should help cut down on some of the tiredness:

~ Wear supportive walking shoes. This isn't the day to cook in bare feet or bedroom slippers.

~ Wear comfortable clothes.

~ Go to bed early the night before.

~ Eat a good breakfast.

~ Remember to stop for lunch (and sit down while you eat).

~ Take frequent mini-breaks.

~ Do as much meal preparation sitting at the kitchen table as possible.

~ Pull up a stool next to the counter and sit whenever you can.

~ Plan a special treat to look forward to afterward: go out to dinner; go on a picnic; take a long, relaxing bath; watch a favorite movie; go to bed early.

~ Tell your spouse you'll make several of his or her favorite meals in exchange for a back rub or foot massage at the end of the day.

Freezing

If possible, lower your freezer's temperature by 10 degrees for 24 hours before your big cooking day. Foods should be frozen at zero-degrees Farenheit, or below, to prevent spoilage and to minimize changes in flavor, texture and nutrients. Set your freezer to -10 degrees F before you start adding large amounts of unfrozen food to your freezer. After food is frozen solid, turn freezer back to zero.

Label all freezer bags and containers with the name of the meal, date frozen, number of servings, heating instructions and any other special preparation instructions (i.e. sprinkle with one cup grated cheese before baking, etc.). Many frozen foods look alike after freezing so don't skip the labeling step. Trust me, you don't want to play "Guess-the-Frozen-Meal" when you're looking for tomorrow's dinner.

Cool food quickly before placing it in the freezer. Don't let food stand at room temperature for longer than 30 minutes. Either set the meal in the refrigerator in a shallow container or place it into a shallow pan in a sink partially filled with ice water. Stir the food frequently during the cooling process. To prevent large ice crystals forming as your meal freezers, food should be no warmer than room temperature when placed into the freezer.

Use good quality durable, leak-proof and moisture-proof freezer bags, foils and plastic containers. This isn't the time to scrimp on packaging. Make sure any plastic containers you use for freezing are food grade plastic. Also, if the labels on packaging material don't indicate the material is made for use in the freezer, it probably isn't. It's no bargain to recycle plastic vegetable or bread bags only to have them leak out your food and hard work.

Remove air from your freezer bags by either pressing the air out with your hands starting at the bottom and working up toward the opening; or using a drinking straw to draw out the excess air before sealing the bag. Removing excess air will prevent freezer burn while also making flatter bags to maximize freezer space. Conserve freezer space by freezing bags flat and then stacking on end. Some cooks freeze large liquid-filled bags inside empty cardboard cereal boxes. When the boxes are removed, you have easy to stack bricks of frozen food.

Prepared meals can be frozen directly in the casserole or baking dishes. If you'll be reheating in the container, be aware that glass dishes can break if put directly into a preheated oven unless the manufacturer specifies the container is safe from freezer to oven. Casserole dishes can be freed for other uses by lining them with heavy-duty aluminum foil before filling. After the product has been baked and frozen, remove from the dish, wrap fully, seal, label and freeze.

Pack freezer containers tightly, without air pockets, but remember to leave head space of at least one-inch to allow liquid-based meals to expand during freezing.

To save time during reheating, consider packaging foods in freezer-to-microwave safe containers.

Tomato-based items and other acidic foods will react with aluminum, eating holes through your foil or aluminum baking pans. Oiling or coating the pans and foil with spray-on cooking oil helps to prevent this problem.

Thawing, Serving and Power Outages

Most main dishes can be reheated either with or without thawing first. If you want to completely thaw the meal first, take the frozen dinner out of your freezer 36 to 48 hours before you need to use it, to assure it's not still frozen when mealtime arrives. Thaw meals in your refrigerator rather than on the counter top to avoid spoilage.

For reheating precooked meals directly from the frozen state, use the temperature setting originally used for cooking the meal. Then cook the meal for slightly less than "double" the original cooking time. For example, if a casserole originally baked for 30 minutes, start with reheating the fully frozen meal for 50 minutes, checking carefully near the end of the cooking time to prevent overcooking. Casseroles are done when the edges are bubbly and the center is hot.

Microwave ovens do an excellent job of reheating. Check your manufacturer's directions for specific instructions and times.

You can thaw frozen food by immersing the freezer bag in a bowl or sink of cold water. Change water frequently.

For quick reheating of frozen sauces or creamy foods, heat in a double boiler. Start with warm, not hot, water in the lower pan to prevent food from sticking and becoming mushy. Partial thawing in the refrigerator will speed up the heating process.

To avoid moisture build up, thaw breaded foods in the refrigerator overnight with the freezer bag opened or removed.

Most baked goods (breads, rolls, muffins, cakes) can be thawed quickly and safely at room temperature (except for fruit pies and any items with cream-based or watery fillings). Keep baked goods wrapped in original packing to prevent drying out and condensation.

If you suffer a power outage, keep your freezer closed. Little or no thawing should occur within the first 12 to 20 hours in a freezer kept at zero-degrees Farenheit.

If your freezer is full of food and the power will be out of order longer than one day, you have two options. You can either move the contents of your freezer to a rental frozen food locker, or you can purchase dry ice for your freezer. If using dry ice, lay cardboard over the packages in your freezer and place dry ice on the cardboard. Never place dry ice directly on to your packages of food, and always wear heavy gloves when handling dry ice. A 50 pound block of dry ice should keep your food frozen for two to three days.

Twelve Additional Cooking Tips

After preparing freezer-meals for several months, you'll start developing short cuts and tricks of your own that make cooking simpler and faster. I've collected a small sampling of assorted helpful tips from experienced freezer-meal cooks to keep in mind as you prepare for your own big cooking day.

~ It's sometimes difficult to pour soup or liquid items into freezer bags. If you open a freezer bag inside of a large coffee can and fold the opening edges of the bag down over the top edges of the can, it's easy to pour soup into the bags. One freezer-meal cook sets up a half dozen coffee cans on her counter, lines the cans with bags and then moves down the counter pouring soup into each can.

~ Double bag soupy items if you're nervous or uncertain of the quality of your freezer bags. You can slip a notecard with the label and reheating instructions between the two bag layers. The outer bag can also be reused many times.

~ Wear short sleeves so you're not dragging your cuffs through spaghetti sauce or taco meat.

~ Keep a small damp kitchen towel hooked to your apron for wiping hands and cleaning small spills easily.

~ Keep hot pads readily available and make certain the pads don't get wet or damp.

~ Keep pets away from your food preparation areas. I've heard horror stories about busy cooks turning around to find a pet eating from a large bowl of meatloaf mix or spaghetti sauce.

~ Professional cooks usually wear a hairnet under their chef's hat to insure that their hair stays out of the food.

~ If you want to keep your frequently used utensils handy, wear an apron with large pockets. Keep your freezer labels and marking pens in the pockets, too. One cook mentioned that she uses a tool belt to hold her large ladle, wooden spoons, wire whisks, etc.

~ For added support for your feet while cooking on your feet all day, try wearing hiking boots or nurses' shoes.

~ If you need to de-bone hot chicken or turkey meat, wear rubber dishwashing gloves.

~ Play upbeat music.

~ To cut down on tears when chopping large quantities of onions, the easiest and most effective thing to do is to use your food processor. Other suggestions include wearing swimming goggles (or welder's goggles), or placing the onions in the freezer for ten to fifteen minutes before chopping. Some of the more unusual tips I've heard, include burning a candle on the counter next to your cutting board, or holding an unlit match stick in your mouth while chopping.

Frozen Assets Preparation Steps
(A Quick Overview)

1) Choose 10 to 15 favorite recipes (depending on how often you're willing to eat the same meal each month). In order to take advantage of sale prices on meats, cheese, etc., check local grocery ads before planing your menu.

2) Use a blank calendar page to plan your meals for the month.

3) Go through your recipes and write down the exact amount of every ingredient. Then go through your cupboards and refrigerator marking off

each item you have in stock. The remaining ingredients will be your shopping list.

4) Figure out what type of freezer containers you will need and how many. Add to your shopping list anything you don't already have on hand (foil, plastic wrap, disposable foil pans, freezer bags, etc.).

5) Clean out your freezer and refrigerator ahead of time to make room for all the food you'll bring home from the grocery store.

6) Go shopping. After you've arrived home, put away all perishable foods in your refrigerator, leaving out canned goods and other items needed for cooking the next day.

7) Separate your recipes according to main protein: chicken, ground beef, dried beans, ham, etc. Plan on preparing the recipes in groups according to main ingredients.

8) Read through your recipes and break them down into steps. Plan to do similar steps together. If you'll need to brown ground beef for tacos, spaghetti sauce and sloppy joes, brown all the meat together, then divide the browned meat when preparing the recipes.

9) Set your freezer to -10 degrees F before you start adding large amounts of unfrozen food to your freezer (it's best to do this the day before cooking).

10) Prepare as many of the ingredients ahead as possible. Decide which things to prepare the evening before (chop vegetables, grate cheese, prepare spaghetti sauce, boil chicken, brown ground beef, etc.).

11) Go to bed early the night before.

12) Eat a good breakfast on cooking day and don't forget to stop for lunch. Take frequent mini-breaks.

13) Dress comfortably, wear supportive shoes, tie back long hair, put on an apron, smile.

14) Assemble all necessary utensils, pots, pans, measuring cups, appliances, etc.

15) Prepare your most complicated recipes early in the day while you're still fresh.

16) While cooking, keep the sink filled with warm, soapy water and wash your pots and pans, measuring cups, spoons and other cooking utensils as you go. Wash hands frequently, especially after handling raw meats.

17) To prevent overcooking (or that warmed-over taste), slightly undercook foods that will be reheated after freezing.

18) Pack food in quantities that will be used for family-sized meals.

19) Label all freezer bags and containers with the name of the meal, date frozen, number of servings, heating instructions and any other special preparation instructions (i.e. sprinkle with one cup grated cheese before baking, etc.).

20) Package grated cheese or crumb toppings in small freezer bags, tape to the main dish container and include instructions on the label for adding the topping before reheating.

21) Remove air from your freezer bags by either pressing the air out with your hands starting at the bottom and working upward or by using a drinking straw to draw out excess air before sealing.

22) Cool food quickly before placing in the freezer. Food should be no warmer than room temperature when put into the freezer. Freeze food quickly to avoid the formation of large ice crystals.

23) Pack freezer containers tightly without air pockets, but remember to leave head space of at least one-inch allowing for the expansion of liquid-based meals.

24) Set meal packages directly on freezer shelves allowing room for air circulation. After the meals are frozen solid, stack them tightly.

So there you have it, the "ins" and "outs" of freezer meal-cooking. Now it's time to put all of these ideas into practice with one of our menu plans—or design your own! The next three chapters will offer meal plans you can easily follow for your first bulk cooking experiences. The sections following the meals plans offer recipes you can use and customize to create your own menus and plans. Whether you try our plans or create your own—happy infrequent cooking!

5

The Thirty-Day Meal Plan

Freezer-meal cooking can actually become a way of life and affect more than just meal preparation. I never have to think twice about providing a meal to someone with a new baby or someone facing difficult circumstances. I don't have to worry about what time we get home from the zoo in order to get dinner prepared on time.

Regularly cooking for the freezer can also alter the way you think about food. Every new recipe I see is automatically sent through my mind's "but will it freeze?" filter. Some freezer-meal cooks have been known to choose recipes strictly because the food would look "pretty" in the freezer bag.

Even the family of the freezer-meal cook can take on a new mind set.

The other night my husband was tucking our seven-year-old son in bed for the night. They were reading a story about frozen Woolly Mammoths found in Siberia. Our son asked, "How'd the Mammoth get frozen, Daddy? Did a hunter shoot it and then freeze the meat to eat later?"

My husband chuckled and said, "Yes, those were the first freezer-meals like Mommy makes—cook for a day, eat for a year!"

We laughed about that for days!

THIRTY-DAY MEAL LINEUP

Spaghetti Sauce
     Sauce over pasta (2 meals)
     Baked Ziti (3 meals)
     Lazy Lasagna (2 meals)
     Meatball Sandwiches (1 meal)

Beef Mixture for Meatloaf and Meatballs
     Meatloaves (2 meals)
     Salisbury Steak (1 meal)
     Sweet-Sour Meatballs (1 meal)
     Chili-Day Meatballs (1 meal)
     (Meatball sandwiches—listed under Spaghetti sauce heading)

Chicken Broccoli
     Served with rice (2 meals)
     Served over noodles (2 meals)

Mexi-Chicken (3 meals)
Broccoli-Ham Bake (2 meals)
Scalloped Potatoes and Ham (4 meals)
Mix-n-Match Chicken Soup (4 meals)

THIRTY-DAY MEAL SHOPPING LIST:

2 pounds Italian bulk sausage
9 pounds ground beef
3 chickens
3 pounds ham

6 onions
2 green peppers
1 bunch celery
4 cloves garlic (or 4-teaspoons garlic)
4 pounds broccoli
5 pounds potatoes
1 cup mushrooms

salt
pepper
thyme
oregano
marjoram
beef bouillon
brown sugar
cornstarch
flour
cider vinegar
lemon juice
soy sauce
vegetable oil
2 packages taco seasonings (or cumin and chili powder)

5 jars (15-ounce) spaghetti sauce

56 ounces tomato sauce

4 (16-ounce) cans Italian-style stewed tomatoes

2 (16-ounce) cans whole kernel corn

1 (4-ounce) can sliced black olives

2 (10-¾ ounce) cans cream of mushroom soup

1 (10-¾ ounce) cans cream of broccoli soup

24 ounces chicken broth

1 (14-ounce) can pineapple tidbits or chunks

1 (5-ounce) can water chestnuts

1 (12-ounce) jar chili sauce

11 ounces grape jelly

Spaghetti noodles (4 meals worth)

3 pounds Ziti (or Penne) pasta

12 ounces lasagna noodles

1½ pound wide egg noodles

2 cups Quaker Quick Barley (or regular)

3 cups dry bread crumbs

3 pounds rice

5 cups mozzarella cheese

¾ cup Parmesan cheese

2 cups small curd cottage cheese (or ricotta)

½ cup sour cream

1½ cups margarine or butter

12 cups milk

4 pounds cheddar cheese

6 Hoagie rolls (or hot dog buns)

7 eggs

2 pounds frozen french fries

THIRTY-DAY MEAL PREPARATION INSTRUCTIONS

The Day Before

~ Shop.

~ Make spaghetti sauce according to recipe. Cool; place sauce in refrigerator overnight.

~ Boil chicken(s) in a large Dutch oven or stock pot with enough water to fully cover the chicken. Add several stalks of celery and some sliced onion. Cook until the meat is white to the bone, and falling off the bone easily. After the chicken is finished cooking, cool slightly and place in refrigerator to cool completely overnight.

~ Chop onions, celery and green pepper. Set aside in separate covered bowls in the refrigerator.

~ Cut broccoli into bite-sized pieces. Keep in refrigerator.

Cooking Day

~ Cook Ziti noodles according to package directions. It's better to undercook the pasta, rather than overcook. The noodles should still be slightly firm, or they will turn to mush after freezing, thawing and reheating.

~ Prepare Baked Ziti according to recipe.

~ Cook barley for Mexi-Chicken.

~ Prepare Lazy Lasagna according to recipe.

~ Bag, label and freeze leftover spaghetti sauce for use in meatball sandwiches and to serve over pasta.

~ Prepare Beef Mixture for Meatloaves and Meatballs according to recipe.

~ Divide mixture in half.

~ Use half to form small (1-inch) meatballs.

~ Use remainder to form two loaves for meatloaf and six thin oval meat patties for Salisbury Steak.

~ Bake meatloaves and cook Salisbury Steak patties according to directions in recipe.

~ Using a spoon, skim fat off top of chicken stock pot; remove chicken from broth; save broth to make soup later; de-bone chicken and cut meatinto bite-sized pieces.

~ Steam broccoli lightly.

~ While broccoli is steaming, prepare Mexi-Chicken according to recipe.

~ Prepare Chicken Broccoli according to recipe.

~ Cut ham into bite-sized pieces.

~ Prepare Broccoli Ham Bake according to recipe.

~ Prepare Scalloped Potatoes and Ham according to recipe.

~ Put stockpot containing chicken broth on stovetop to boil.

~ Using chicken broth, prepare "Mix-n-Match Soup" adding any leftover vegetables, meats, grains, or pastas. If you need more liquid, use one chicken bouillon cube per 1½ cups added water.

~ Let soup cook while you're cleaning the kitchen.

~ Allow soup to cool; pour soup into labeled freezer bags; freeze. (Double bag for security.)

FROZEN ASSETS

BULK SPAGHETTI SAUCE
(36 servings)

This sauce will be used in this meal plan for sauce over pasta, Lazy Lasagna, Baked Ziti and Meatball Sandwiches.

2 pounds Italian sausage
2 cups onions, chopped
½ cup green pepper, chopped
½ cup celery, chopped
2 teaspoons garlic, minced
5 jars commercial spaghetti sauce (or 12 cups homemade sauce)
4 16-ounce cans Italian-style stewed tomatoes, cut up, undrained
1 large can sliced black olives

Brown sausage, onion, green pepper, celery and garlic in large Dutch oven or stock pot. Add spaghetti sauce and stewed tomatoes. Simmer on low to medium heat for at least one hour. Stir occasionally. Add black olives after simmering. Allow to cool. Set aside sauce needed for other recipes and freeze the rest in bags for sauce over pasta meals.

LAZY LASAGNA
(10 servings)

When preparing lasagna for the freezer there's no need to precook the noodles.

12 ounces lasagna noodles, uncooked
5-6 cups spaghetti sauce
2 cups cream-style cottage cheese, or ricotta
12 ounces Mozzarella cheese, sliced or grated
½ cup grated Parmesan cheese

In two greased 10x6x2-inch baking dishes, make layers in the following order: half each noodles, cottage cheese, Mozzarella slices, spaghetti sauce, and sprinkled Parmesan cheese. Repeat. Make certain the dry noodles are completely covered by sauce. Wrap pans completely with foil; label and freeze.

(To make this meal incredibly rich, add one 8-ounce package cream cheese. Pinch off nickel-sized portions of cream cheese and plop evenly over lasagna just before adding the second layer of uncooked pasta.)

To Serve:
To thaw, take meal from freezer at least 24 hours before serving. Place in refrigerator. Bake tightly covered at 350° for about 45 minutes, or until edges are bubbly and center is hot. Take cover off during final 10 minutes of cooking time. Let stand 10 minutes before serving.

BAKED ZITI
(18 servings)

This is one of those recipes my family never seems to eat often enough. Everyone loves it, even my three-year-old. "More yummy noodles, Mommy!"

3 pounds Ziti (or Penne) pasta
1 pound ground beef (optional)
1 cup onion, chopped
1 cup green pepper, chopped
2 jars commercial spaghetti sauce (or 6 cups homemade)
3 cups Mozzarella cheese, grated
¾ cup grated Parmesan cheese (to be used at serving time—not during initial prep)

note: Three cups Ground Meat Mixture (see page 66) can be substituted for ground beef, chopped onion and green pepper.

Cook pasta until just barely tender; drain thoroughly and rinse with cold water to stop cooking process. Brown ground beef; drain. Add onion and green pepper to meat and sauté until vegetables are softened (if needed, add small amount of olive oil during sauté process). Add spaghetti sauce. Combine sauce and cooked pasta; mix well. Divide sauce and pasta mixture into three gallon-sized freezer bags; label. Divide grated mozzarella cheese into three quart-sized freezer bags; attach to pasta bags. Freeze.

To Serve:
Thaw. Spread pasta into 9x13-inch baking pan. Sprinkle mozzarella evenly over pasta. Sprinkle ¼ cup Parmesan cheese over top. Cover dish and bake for 30 minutes at 350°, or until bubbly on the edges and hot in the middle. Remove foil and bake five more minutes.

BEEF MIX FOR MEATLOAF AND MEATBALLS

2 meatloaves

1 Salisbury Steak

3 meals of meatballs

~ Sweet-Sour Meatballs

~ Chili-Day Meatballs

~ Meatball Sandwiches (also listed under spaghetti sauce)

24 ounces tomato sauce

3 cups dry bread crumbs

7 eggs, lightly beaten

1 cup onion, finely chopped

½ cup green pepper, finely chopped

2 teaspoons salt, optional

¼ teaspoon dried thyme, crushed

¼ teaspoon dried marjoram, crushed

8 pounds ground beef

Combine first eight ingredients. Add ground beef and mix well. Divide meat mixture in half.

For Meatloaf:

Shape half the meat mixture into three loaves and place in a large high-sided baking dish. Don't allow the loaves to touch while baking. Bake at 350° for 1 hour. Cool; wrap in heavy-duty foil; label and freeze. To serve, thaw loaves and bake in 350° oven for 30 minutes or until heated through.

For Meatballs:

Shape into meatballs (use small cookie scoop if available) and place on broiler pan so grease can drain while cooking. Bake uncovered in 350° oven for 30 minutes. Divide into meal-sized portions. To prevent from freezing into a solid meatball-mass, freeze individually on cookie sheets and then place in freezer bags. Label and freeze. To serve, thaw and reheat with your choice of sauces.

<u>For Salisbury Steak:</u>

Form meat mixture into oval ½-inch thick patties. Heat nonstick skillet over medium heat until hot. Place beef patty in skillet; cook seven to eight minutes or until centers are no longer pink, turning once. Cool; place in freezer bags; freeze. Thaw; heat with 1 (10¾-ounce) can cream of mushroom soup poured over as sauce; serve with rice or noodles.

The following recipes are various ways to use frozen meatballs. The sauces require some preparation, but the meals go together quickly with your stockpile of precooked meatballs in the freezer.

SWEET-SOUR MEATBALLS
(5 servings)

1 (14-ounce) can pineapple tidbits or chunks, undrained

¼ cup brown sugar

2 tablespoons cornstarch

½ cup water

¼ cup cider vinegar

1 teaspoon soy sauce (or more to taste)

1 family meal-sized portion of freezer meatballs

1 (5-ounce) can water chestnuts, drained and thinly sliced

1 green pepper, cut in strips

Drain pineapple tidbits, reserving syrup. In medium saucepan, combine brown sugar and cornstarch. Blend in reserved syrup, water, cider vinegar and soy sauce. Cook and stir over low heat until thick and bubbly. Carefully stir in meatballs, water chestnuts, green pepper strips and pineapple. Heat to boiling. Serve over hot cooked rice.

CHILI-DAY MEATBALLS
(5 servings)

1 (12-ounce) jar chili sauce (or 1½ cups homemade)
11 ounces grape jelly
2 tablespoons lemon juice
1 cube beef bouillon dissolved in ½ cup water
1 family meal-sized portion of freezer meatballs

Whisk together chili sauce, grape jelly, lemon juice and bouillon breaking up all clumps. Simmer on low heat until sauce starts to thicken. Add freezer meatballs; cook in sauce until meatballs are fully thawed and heated through. Serve over cooked noodles or rice.

Crockpot Method:

Mix together sauce as described above. Place frozen meatballs in crockpot, pouring sauce over them. Stir gently to coat. Cook for eight hours on a low setting.

MEATBALL SANDWICHES
(6 servings)

1 family size serving of meatballs (approximately 4-5 meatballs
   per person)
6 hot dog buns or hoagie rolls
6 thin slices mozzarella cheese
2 cups spaghetti sauce

Thaw meatballs and spaghetti sauce. Heat until hot. Place meatballs into warmed buns. Ladle small amount of spaghetti sauce on to each sandwich; place mozzarella slice on to each sandwich.

MEXI-CHICKEN
(18 servings)

2 cups onion, chopped

2 cloves garlic (or more to taste), minced

2 tablespoons vegetable oil

4 cups water

2 cups Quaker Quick barley (regular barley can be used, but cooking
time increases dramatically)

2 (16-ounce) cans chopped tomatoes, undrained

2 (16-ounce) cans tomato sauce

3 cups chicken broth

2 (16-ounce) cans whole kernel corn, drained

6 cups cooked chicken, chopped or shredded

Spices:

Either use 2 tablespoons chili powder and 1 teaspoon cumin *or* use 2
packages taco seasonings

In large Dutch oven, cook onion and garlic in oil until tender. Add all
ingredients except chicken. Bring to boil. Reduce heat and simmer 10
minutes, stirring occasionally. Add cooked chicken; continue simmering for
another 10 minutes, or until chicken is heated through and barley is tender.
Cool; spoon into freezer bags; label and freeze.

If you're using regular barley, rather than the quick cooking variety,
you'll need to cook the barley ahead of time. Allow one hour for barley to
cook. Check directions on your barley.

To Serve:

Thaw chicken mixture. Heat in skillet until hot. Serve over corn tortilla
chips or scoop into flour tortillas fajita-style.

CHICKEN BROCCOLI
(16 servings)

1 cup margarine
1 cup flour
8 cups milk
Salt and pepper to taste
4 cups cooked chicken, chopped
2 pounds broccoli, steamed
2 pounds cheddar cheese, grated

Make white sauce: melt margarine in a large heavy pan. Add flour, stirring constantly. When mixture reaches the boiling point, add milk, mixing constantly with a wire whisk. Heat until almost boiling, stirring constantly. Remove from heat. Place cooked chicken into four 8x8-inch baking pans. Divide steamed broccoli and place over chicken. Pour white sauce over all. Sprinkle each pan with grated cheese. Cover pans with foil; label and freeze. This recipe can also be frozen in zip-top freezer bags to conserve space in your freezer. If storing in bags, divide grated cheese among smaller freezer bags and freeze separately from the chicken and broccoli.

To Serve:
Thaw. Bake at 350° for 30 minutes. Serve over cooked rice or spaghetti noodles for a Tetrazinni-type meal.

BROCCOLI-HAM BAKE
(12 servings)

4 cups broccoli, cooked and chopped

2 pounds frozen french fries

1 (10¾-ounce) can cream of mushroom soup

1 (10¾-ounce) can cream of broccoli soup

2 cups milk

2-3 cups ham, cubed

2 cups yellow cheese (any variety), grated

Spread frozen french fries in two greased (or sprayed) 9x13-inch baking dishes. Sprinkle chopped broccoli over fries. In a separate bowl, blend soups and milk; stir in ham; pour over fries and broccoli. Wrap baking dish; label and freeze. Place grated cheese in two small freezer bags and attach to baking dish with Broccoli-Ham Bake.

<u>To Serve:</u>

Thaw. Sprinkle grated cheese over top of casserole. Bake at 350° for 25-30 minutes.

SCALLOPED POTATOES AND HAM
(20 servings)

The potatoes will start to turn brown if you don't get them right into the bags with the sauce, so move quickly when preparing this meal.

1 pound ham, in small cubes
5 pounds potatoes, sliced with skin on
1 large onion, chopped
1 pound yellow cheese (any variety), grated
½ cup margarine
½ cup flour
4 cups milk
Salt and pepper to taste

For sauce: melt margarine in heavy pan. Add flour, stirring constantly. Heat to boiling point; add milk; mix constantly with wire whisk. Heat until thickened, stirring constantly. Add spices. In separate pan, sauté meat with onions. Boil sliced potatoes, but remove from heat while still firm. Divide potatoes between five freezer bags. Divide ham and onion mixture, and add to potatoes in freezer bags. Divide white sauce and pour over meat and potatoes in freezer bags. Label and freeze quickly. Divide grated cheese between smaller freezer bags, attatch and freeze.

To Serve:
Thaw potato mixture. Pour into baking pan. Sprinkle with grated cheese. Bake at 350° for 20 minutes, or until heated through.

MIX-N-MATCH CHICKEN SOUP
(10 servings)

10 cups chicken broth *or* 4 chicken bouillon cubes dissolved in 10 cups water.

Chopped and cooked chicken or turkey

Grain ~ Choose one or two (2 cups)
  Rice, cooked (any variety)
  Barley, cooked
  Pasta, raw
  Corn
  Dumplings (add at end of cooking time)

Vegetables ~ Choose two or more
(1- 2 cups ~ sliced, diced or shredded)
  Carrots
  Celery
  Cabbage
  Onion
  Potatoes
  Tomatoes
  Green Beans
  Yellow "Wax" Beans
  Turnips
  Parsnips
  Corn
  Zucchini
  Green Pepper
  Peas or pea pods

Cauliflower

Broccoli

Whatever you have around

<u>Seasonings ~ Choose two to four</u> (1 - 2 teaspoons each)

Basil

Cayenne (dash)

Chives

Cumin

Garlic

Marjoram

Oregano

Parsley

Rosemary

Thyme

Onion powder

<u>To prepare soup:</u>

Bring stock to boil in large stock pot or Dutch oven. Add all ingredients; salt and pepper to taste; reduce heat; simmer for at least one hour.

To Freeze:

Allow soup to cool. Pour into freezer bags and freeze.

notes: using a liquid measure to scoop soup from pot while holding a freezer bag over the pot, works well when the pot is full and heavy. Or line coffee cans or other meal-size containers with a freezer bag and pour directly into bag. Seal; remove from container, and freeze.

If using noodles or rice, add these items after removing the soup from the stove. Or store these items and add when meal is thawed and being prepared. This will avoid noodles and rice becoming too mushy.

6

The Two-Week Meal Plan

With day-to-day schedules being so varied, there are many reasons people use a two-week meal plan. Sometimes your designated cooking day may not allow for six or seven hours worth of preparation. If that should happen the two-week plan offers a nice alternative of only two or three hours of preparation.

When money is tight a two-week menu may be more plausible than cooking for a full month. A shortage of storage space is another reason people use the two-week plan. And for some, it's just plain easier to follow. For whatever the reason you chose the two-week meal plan, get ready to enjoy the benefits of bulk-cooking!

TWO-WEEK MEAL LINEUP

<u>All-Purpose Ground Meat Mix</u>
    Stuffed Peppers (2 meals)
    Sloppy Joes (1 meal)
    Texas-Style Chili (2 meals)
    Poor Man's Casserole (1 meal)
    Spaghetti Pie (1 meal)

Black Beans and Rice (2 meals)

Chicken Curry (2 meals)
    Serve with East Indian Rice Ring

Broccoli Quiche (1 meal)

Lentil-Rice Soup (2 meals)

SHOPPING LIST FOR TWO-WEEK PLAN

5 pounds ground meat (beef or turkey)
1 chicken

1 pound broccoli
2 apples
8 medium potatoes
5 cups celery
6 cloves of garlic
7 onions
13 large green peppers
7 cloves of garlic
lettuce
tomato
40 ounces salsa

chili powder
oregano
cumin
salt
pepper
paprika
curry powder
nutmeg
brown sugar
cornstarch
soy sauce

7 eggs
6 cups cheddar cheese

Parmesan cheese

1 cup cottage cheese

1 cup sour cream

1 cup butter or margarine

7 cups milk

64 ounces tomato juice

32 ounces tomato sauce

1 (6-ounce) can tomato paste

3 (10¾-ounce) cans tomato soup

4 (16-ounce) cans crushed tomatoes

1 (16-ounce) can Italian-style stewed tomatoes

4 (16-ounce) cans red kidney beans

2 (16-ounce) cans black beans

3 (16-ounce) cans corn

2 (3-ounce) cans sliced mushrooms

2 cups uncooked lentils

6 ounces dry spaghetti noodles

3 pounds rice (long grain)

prepared mustard

¼ cup slivered almonds

½ cup light raisins

shredded coconut

6 hamburger buns

1 pound frozen mixed vegetables

20 ounces frozen corn

TWO-WEEK PLAN PREPARATION INSTRUCTIONS

DAY BEFORE

~ Shop.

~ Boil chicken. Allow to cool and then place pot with chicken and cooking water into refrigerator overnight.

~ Chop celery, onions and one green pepper (reserving other peppers whole for Stuffed Peppers recipe.)

~ Cut up broccoli into bite-sized pieces.

COOKING DAY

~ Cook rice to make four cups.

~ While rice is cooking, boil spaghetti noodles (for Spaghetti Pie) according to package directions. Cook until just tender but not soft. Rinse pasta in cold water to stop cooking process.

~ Peel potatoes. Boil until soft. Mash and cool. Place in refrigerator until preparing Poor Man's Casserole.

~ Prepare All-Purpose Ground Meat Mix according to recipe.

~ Prepare Sloppy Joes according to recipe.

~ Prepare Stuffed Peppers according to recipe.

~ Prepare Texas-Style Chili according to recipe.

~ Prepare Poor Man's Casserole according to recipe.

~ Prepare Spaghetti Pie according to recipe.

~ Prepare Broccoli Quiche according to recipe.

~ Prepare Black Beans and Rice according to recipe.

~ Prepare Lentil-Rice Soup according to recipe.

~ Remove chicken from refrigerator. Skim fat off top of broth with a spoon. Remove chicken meat from bones reserving broth.

~ Prepare Chicken Curry according to recipe.

~ If there is chicken broth and meat leftover at this point, prepare Mix-n-Match Soup (page 58) while cleaning your cooking area.

RECIPES
FOR
THE TWO-WEEK
MEAL PLAN

ALL-PURPOSE GROUND MEAT MIX
(Makes about 12 cups)

5 pounds ground meat (beef or turkey)
2 cups celery, chopped
1 clove garlic, minced
2 cups onion, chopped
1 cup green pepper, diced
½ teaspoon pepper
1 teaspoon salt (optional)

In a large pot, brown ground beef. Drain. Stir in celery, garlic, onion, green pepper, salt and pepper; cover and simmer about 10 minutes, until vegetables are tender but not soft.

SLOPPY JOES
(4-6 servings)

2 cups All-Purpose Ground Meat Mixture (page 66)
1 (10¾-ounce) can tomato soup
2 tablespoons brown sugar
1 teaspoon prepared mustard

Place Ground Meat Mixture into large skillet. Add tomato soup, brown sugar and mustard; stir. Heat covered over medium-low heat, and simmer 10 minutes. Freeze.

<u>To Serve:</u>

Thaw and heat Sloppy Joe mix in skillet. Serve ladled on to hamburger buns.

STUFFED PEPPERS
(12 servings)

12 large green peppers
2 cups All-Purpose Ground Meat Mix (page 66)
2 teaspoons paprika
2 cups cooked rice (long-grain is best, but use what you have)
4 cloves garlic, minced
24 ounces tomato sauce
2 (10¾-ounce) cans tomato soup (save until serving day)

Cut off tops of green peppers; remove seeds. Mix together Ground Meat Mix, rice, spices and tomato sauce. Stuff meat and rice mixture into green peppers. Place in roasting pan. Bake covered at 350° for 40 minutes. Cool. Wrap individually in foil; label and freeze.

To Serve:

Unwrap stuffed peppers. Place in roasting pan. Pour tomato soup over peppers. Heat at 350° for 25 minutes. Or unwrap and cook in microwave oven.

TEXAS-STYLE CHILI
(12 servings)

4 cups All-Purpose Ground Beef Mixture (page 66)
2 packages taco seasonings (or 2 tablespoons chili powder plus 2
   tablespoons ground cumin)
2 teaspoons salt (optional)
4 (16-ounce) cans crushed tomatoes, undrained
4 (16-ounce) cans red kidney beans, drained (or use home prepared
   beans)
3 cans corn

Place all ingredients into large pot. Bring to a boil. Reduce heat and simmer for at least one hour, stirring occasionally. Cool chili. Put into freezer bags; label and freeze.

To Serve:

Thaw in covered saucepan over low heat. After thawed, increase heat and cook until chili is hot.

POOR MAN'S CASSEROLE
(6 servings)

2 cups All-Purpose Ground Beef Mixture (page 66)
1 pound frozen vegetables (your choice, any combination)
spices (whatever you like: marjoram, parsley, Italian spice, ground
pepper, etc.)
3 cups mashed potatoes
1 cup yellow cheese, grated

Mix meat with vegetables and place in 9x13-inch casserole dish. Add spices. Spread mashed potatoes over top of meat and vegetable mixture. Sprinkle grated cheese over top of potatoes. Wrap casserole in foil; label and freeze.

To Serve:
Thaw. Heat uncovered in 350° oven for 20-30 minutes, or until heated through.

SPAGHETTI PIE
(6 servings)

6 ounces dry spaghetti noodles

2 tablespoons butter or margarine

½ cup Parmesan cheese

2 well beaten eggs

½ pound ground beef

½ cup chopped onion

1 (8-ounce) can Italian-style stewed tomatoes, undrained

1 (6-ounce) can tomato paste

1 teaspoon sugar

1 teaspoon dried oregano, crushed

½ clove garlic, minced

1 cup cottage cheese

½ cup shredded cheese (your choice: mozzarella, cheddar, American, Monteray Jack)

Cook spaghetti noodles. Drain. Stir margarine into hot noodles until melted. Stir in Parmesan cheese and eggs. Form pasta mixture into a crust-shape in a buttered 9-inch pie plate. In skillet, cook ground beef and onions until meat is browned. Drain. Add tomatoes, tomato paste, sugar, oregano and garlic. Heat through. Spread cottage cheese over bottom of spaghetti crust. Top with tomato and meat mixture. Sprinkle grated cheese over all. Cover pie pan with foil; label and freeze.

To Serve:

Thaw. Bake, covered, for 25 minutes at 350°. Remove foil and bake for five more minutes or until cheese is lightly browned.

BROCCOLI QUICHE
(6 servings)

Crust:

   1-2 cups rice, cooked (white or brown)

   1 egg, beaten

   1 teaspoon soy sauce

Filling:

   1-2 cups cooked broccoli, cut up

   4 eggs, beaten

   1½ cups milk, or light cream

   1 cup cheese, grated (your choice of Swiss, cheddar, American, etc.)

   ½ teaspoon salt (optional)

   1/8 teaspoon pepper

   Dash of nutmeg or ground mace

Crust:

Mix together cooked rice, egg and soy sauce. Spread evenly to cover well-buttered quiche pan or pie plate. Bake rice crust at 350° for 10 minutes. Remove from oven.

Filling:

Place broccoli in bottom of crust. Mix together: eggs, milk, salt, pepper and nutmeg. Pour over broccoli. Top with grated cheese. Bake at 350° for 45 minutes, or until set. Remove from oven; cool; wrap pie pan; label and freeze.

note: Consider freezing single slices. These make great lunches and can be served hot or cold.

BLACK BEANS AND RICE
(8 servings)

2 cans black beans, drained (or use cooked dry beans)

20 ounces frozen corn

2 cups long grain rice, uncooked (white or brown)

32 ounces salsa (choose your heat—mild, medium or hot)

3 cups tomato juice

½ teaspoon cumin

½ teaspoon oregano

2 cups cheddar cheese, grated

In large bowl, combine all ingredients (except cheese). Pour into two casserole dishes; bake covered at 375° for one hour. Remove from oven. Cool; wrap, label and freeze. Divide grated cheese into two small freezer bags and attach to Black Beans and Rice in freezer.

To Serve:

Thaw. Sprinkle grated cheese over beans and rice; reheat at 350° for 15-20 minutes until cheese is melted and beans and rice are heated through.

LENTIL-RICE SOUP
(10 servings)

1 (12-ounce) can tomato paste
2 (16-ounce) cans tomatoes with juice
8 cups water
2 cups uncooked lentils
2 cups uncooked rice
2 medium onions, chopped
1 cup celery, chopped
2 cloves garlic, minced
Salt and pepper to taste

Put tomato paste and canned tomatoes into large Dutch oven or stock pot. Add water. Stir in all other ingredients. Heat to boiling. Turn down heat and simmer for one hour, or until lentils are soft and rice is cooked. Cool; pour into labeled freezer bags. Freeze.

note: using a liquid measure to scoop soup from pot while holding a freezer bag over the pot, works well when the pot is full and heavy. Or line coffee cans or other meal-size containers with a freezer bag and pour directly into bag. Seal; remove from container, and freeze.

CHICKEN CURRY
(10 servings)

2 tablespoons butter
2 cups pared apple, finely chopped
2 cups celery, sliced
1 cup onion, chopped
2 cloves garlic, minced
4 tablespoons cornstarch
4 to 6 teaspoons curry powder (to taste)
1 teaspoon salt (optional)
1½ cups cold chicken broth
4 cups milk
4 cups cooked chicken, diced
2 (3-ounce) cans sliced mushrooms, drained (or 1 cup sliced fresh)

In saucepan, melt butter; add apple, celery, onion and garlic. Cook until onion is tender. In separate bowl, combine cornstarch, curry, salt and broth. Stir into onion and apple mixture; add milk. Cook and stir until mixture thickens and bubbles. Stir in chicken and mushrooms. Heat through. Divide into freezer bags; label and freeze.

To Serve:
Thaw. In saucepan, heat thoroughly. Serve Chicken Curry over hot cooked rice and pass condiments—raisins, shredded coconut, chopped peanuts, chutney; or serve in East-Indian Rice Ring (page 76).

EAST-INDIAN RICE RING
Prepare on serving day.

¼ cup butter
½ cup onion, chopped
¼ cup slivered almonds
½ cup light raisins
6 cups hot cooked rice
shredded coconut (optional)

In skillet, melt butter and sauté chopped onion and almonds until golden. Add light raisins; heat until plump. Add hot rice; mix gently. Press mixture into greased 6½ cup ring mold. Remove from mold at once and place on to a round serving platter. Fill center of rice ring with Chicken Curry (page 75). Top with a sprinkling of shredded coconut, if desired.

Ten-Day Holiday Meal Plan

Could you imagine a relaxed Christmas and New Year without needing to cook any main dinner recipes—only side dishes and desserts? If that sounds like a great gift to give yourself this year, plan ahead this holiday season using our Ten-Day Holiday Meal Plan.

This meal plan covers the main dish dinner recipes from just before Christmas until New Year's Day. Many people find they need larger amounts of food during this time of year due to guests, unexpected visitors or college-age children returning home for the holidays. If these recipes prepare more than you'll be needing, you can serve leftovers for lunches, or divide the recipes into additional freezer pans and stretch the meals out for a longer period of time.

These recipes include main dishes for a holiday dinner of turkey; several meals of planned turkey leftovers; a breakfast casserole that can be served on Christmas or New Year's morning; and recipes that could be used for company meals throughout the holidays.

Now that you can plan ahead and get your cooking out of the way, get ready to relax and enjoy the holidays!

TEN-DAY HOLIDAY MEAL LINEUP

Turkey Dinner (serves however many you need)

Turkey-Rice (serves 8)

Turkey Stuffed Manicotti (serves 12)

Turkey Noodle Soup (serves 8 - 10)

Ground Beef Mixture
~ Texas-Style Chili (serves 12)
~ Easy Taco Salads (serves 6 - 8)

Spaghetti Sauce
~ Baked Ziti (serves 18)
~ Lasagna (serves 10)
~ Sauce over pasta (serves 10)

Broccoli and Ham Bake (serves 12)

Ham and Cheese Quiche (serves 24)

Holiday Breakfast Casserole (serves 8)

HOLIDAY MEAL PLAN SHOPPING LIST

turkey (figure out weight needed using instructions
     in the turkey dinner recipe on page 84)
2 pounds Italian sausage
ham (2-3 pound)
2½ pounds ground beef (or turkey)
1 pound bulk sausage

8 onions
6 carrots
1 large bunch celery
2 green peppers
4 cups broccoli
lettuce (one head)
2 tomatoes
1 bunch green onions

olive oil
bay leaves
salt
pepper
sage
thyme
garlic
oregano
2 packages taco seasoning (or cumin and chili powder)
parsley
rosemary
dry mustard

7 (15-ounce) jars commercial spaghetti sauce
64 ounces Italian-style stewed tomatoes
2 (4-ounce) cans sliced black olives
5 (10¾-ounce) cream of mushroom soup
1 (10¾-ounce) cream of broccoli soup
16 ounces salsa
64 ounces crushed tomatoes
64 ounces red kidney beans
32 ounces tomato sauce

16 ounces lasagna noodles
16 manicotti shells
12 ounce wide egg noodles
2 pounds Ziti or Penne pasta (medium sized tubes)

white wine (2 cups)

5 cups yellow cheese
2 cups cottage cheese
5 cups mozzarella cheese
3 cups Parmesan cheese
2 cups ricotta cheese
7 eggs

6 ounces frozen peas
2 pounds frozen french fries
one large bag corn chips or tortilla chips
rice
bread

heavy-duty wide aluminum foil

HOLIDAY PLAN PREPARATION INSTRUCTIONS
[will take three half days including shopping]

DAY ONE

~ Shop.

~ Make spaghetti sauce according to recipe. Cool; place sauce in refrigerator overnight.

~ Peel and quarter three onions.

~ Cut six celery stalks into 2-inch pieces.

~ Cut two carrots into 2-inch pieces.

~ Chop remaining onion, celery and green pepper. Set aside chopped vegetables in separate covered bowls in the refrigerator.

~ Cut broccoli into bite-sized pieces. Keep in refrigerator.

~ Dice ham. Keep refrigerated.

~ Cook 4-5 cups rice. Put in fridge.

DAY TWO

~ First thing in the morning, prepare and cook turkey according to recipe. After roasting, put into refrigerator overnight covered with foil.

~ After turkey goes into the oven to bake, prepare Ziti (or Penne) noodles according to package directions. Slightly undercook the pasta. Rinse with cold water to stop cooking process. Drain.

~ While Ziti is boiling, prepare Lazy Lasagna according to recipe. Freeze.

~ Prepare Baked Ziti according to recipe. Freeze.

~ Pour remaining spaghetti sauce into two labeled freezer bags. Freeze.

~ Prepare Ground Meat Mixture according to recipe.

~ While browning Ground Meat Mixture, prepare Broccoli-Ham Bake according to recipe. Freeze.

~ After Ground Meat Mixture is browned and drained, divide into two portions: 2 cups of mixture into a large skillet and the remaining 4 cups into a Dutch oven or stockpot.

~ Prepare skillet Meat Mixture as taco filling for Taco Salads. Label and freeze.

~ Prepare other half as Texas-Style Chili according to recipe. Freeze.

~ Prepare Ham and Cheese Quiche. Freeze.

~ Cook Manicotti shells in boiling salted water until just barely tender. Rinse in cold water. Carefully place Manicotti shells into a shallow pan. Cover; place in fridge overnight.

DAY THREE

~ Remove turkey from fridge. Carefully slice turkey to prepare for turkey dinner meal. Freeze sliced turkey according to recipe instructions. Be sure to retain eight cups of diced turkey for the planned "leftover" recipes. Any additional turkey meat can be used in the Turkey Noodle Soup recipe on page 99.

~ Remove all meat from bones.

~ Begin preparing soup broth. After meat has been removed from bones, place bones and assorted remaining pieces into a large stockpot or Dutch oven. Fill pot with enough water to completely cover the turkey bones and pieces. Add several stalks of celery. Heat to boiling. Turn down heat and simmer for at least one hour.

~ While bones are simmering, prepare Turkey-Rice according to recipe. Freeze.

~ Prepare Turkey-Stuffed Manicotti according to recipe. Freeze.

~ Prepare Holiday Breakfast Casserole according to recipe. Freeze.

~ Remove turkey broth from heat. Using a slotted spoon or small mesh strainer, strain out meat (reserving meat in a separate bowl), bones, celery, etc. Place strained broth in refrigerator to cool. When cool and fat has congealed on top, scoop off fat with a spoon.

~ Prepare Turkey Noodle Soup according to recipe. Cool and freeze.

RECIPES
FOR
THE TEN-DAY HOLIDAY
MEAL PLAN

TURKEY DINNER

You'll need a minimum 6-pound turkey for using in the leftover turkey recipes. For the main turkey dinner, add ¾ pound per person to the 6 pounds already required for the leftover recipes.

Number of People = Weight of Turkey Needed to Buy

6 people   = 10½ pounds
8 people   = 12 pounds
10 people = 13½ pounds
12 people = 15 pounds
14 people = 16½ pounds
16 people = 18 pounds
18 people = 19½ pounds
20 people = 21 pounds

To Prepare Turkey:
3 onions, quartered
6 celery stalks, cut into two-inch pieces
2 medium carrots, cut into two-inch pieces
2 bay leaves
1½ cups white wine (or water)
1 tablespoon olive oil
2 teaspoons salt
2 teaspoons pepper
2 teaspoons sage
1 teaspoon thyme
canned chicken broth, 1 cup per pound (reserve until time to freeze meat)

In bottom of deep roasting pan, place two quartered onions, four celery stalks, carrots, bay leaves and white wine. Remove turkey giblets; rinse bird inside and out. Pat dry with paper towels. Stuff turkey loosely with remaining quartered onion and celery stalks. Brush turkey with olive oil mixed with salt, pepper, sage and thyme. Cover turkey loosely with a large sheet of foil coated lightly with olive oil, crimping foil on to edges of roasting pan. Cook according to chart below. During last 45 minutes, cut band of skin or string between legs and tail. Uncover and continue roasting until done. Baste if desired.

Turkey Roasting Chart (loosely wrapped with foil)
12 - 16 lbs / 325° / 4 - 5 hours
16 - 20 lbs / 325° / 5 - 6 hours
20 - 24 lbs / 325° / 6 - 7 hours

Testing for doneness:
About 20 minutes before roasting time is completed, test bird. Skin on thickest part of drumstick should feel soft when squeezed between fingers, drumstick should move up and down easily and meat thermometer inserted into thickest part of leg should read 185°. (Or follow manufacturer's instructions.)

Freezing Instructions:
Pour liquid and drippings from roasting pan into a bowl. Remove vegetables. Allow to cool in fridge until fat congeals on top. Scoop off fat with a spoon and pour drippings into a labeled freezer bag. Thaw to use for making gravy on serving day.

Allow turkey to cool in pan for about ½ hour; then place turkey and its roasting pan into refrigerator. Allow to cool completely (several hours). When fully chilled, slice turkey as usual. Remove all meat from bones. Place breast and dark meat slices into labeled freezer bags. Pour chicken broth into bags over the meat. Freeze. Be sure to retain 8 cups diced turkey meat for the "leftover" recipes.

To Serve:

Thaw bag of meat and broth and place into a covered baking dish for 30 minutes at 350 F. Or place turkey and broth into a microwave safe dish, cover with plastic wrap and heat until hot (the time will vary with different microwaves, so check manufacturer's directions). Drain off broth (reserve to make more gravy, if needed). Arrange the heated turkey slices attractively on platter. Serve.

GRAVY INSTRUCTIONS:
(12 servings)

2 tablespoons butter, margarine or ½ cup white wine
1/3 cup flour
½ teaspoon salt (optional)
3 cups thawed turkey drippings (If needed, add additional water, chicken broth, or white wine to equal 3 cups)

In a medium saucepan melt butter; thoroughly stir in flour (and salt, if used). Heat over low medium-low heat until bubbling, stirring constantly. Slowly pour liquid into flour and butter mixture, stirring constantly. Continue stirring and increase heat to medium. Continue stirring until gravy boils. Reduce heat to low and simmer an additional two minutes, stirring frequently.

BULK SPAGHETTI SAUCE
(36 servings)

2 pounds Italian sausage
2 cups onions, chopped
½ cup green pepper, chopped
½ cup celery, chopped
2 teaspoons garlic, minced
5 jars (15-ounce) commercial spaghetti sauce (or 12 cups homemade sauce)
4 (16-ounce) cans Italian-style stewed tomatoes, cut up, undrained
1 large can sliced black olives

Brown sausage, onion, green pepper, celery and garlic in large Dutch oven or stock pot. Add spaghetti sauce and stewed tomatoes. Simmer on low to medium heat for at least one hour. Stir occasionally. Add black olives after simmering. Allow to cool.

LAZY LASAGNA
(10 servings)

When preparing lasagna for the freezer there's no need to precook the noodles. If you layer the casserole with dry noodles ensuring your noodles are completely covered with sauce, the noodles will cook during the freezing and baking process absorbing the sauce.

12 ounces lasagna noodles, uncooked
½ teaspoon dried oregano
6 cups spaghetti sauce
2 cups cream-style small curd cottage cheese, or Ricotta
12 ounces mozzarella cheese, sliced or grated
½ cup grated Parmesan cheese

Stir oregano into spaghetti sauce. In two greased 10x6x2-inch baking dishes, make layers in the following order: half each noodles, cottage cheese, Mozzarella slices, spaghetti sauce, and sprinkled Parmesan cheese. Repeat. Make certain the dry noodles are completely covered by sauce. Wrap pans completely with foil; label and freeze.

(To make this meal incredibly rich, add one 8-ounce package cream cheese. Pinch off nickel-sized portions of cream cheese and plop evenly over lasagna just before adding the second layer of uncooked pasta.)

To Serve:
To thaw, take meal from freezer at least 24 hours before serving. Place in refrigerator. Bake tightly covered at 350° for about 45 minutes, or until edges are bubbly and center is hot. Take cover off during final 10 minutes of cooking time. Let stand 10 minutes before serving.

BAKED ZITI
(18 servings)

3 pounds Ziti (or Penne) pasta
1 pound ground beef (optional)
1 cup onion, chopped
1 cup green pepper, chopped
2 jars commercial spaghetti sauce (or 6 cups homemade)
3 cups mozzarella cheese, grated
¾ cup grated Parmesan cheese (to be used at serving time—not during initial prep)

note: Three cups Ground Meat Mixture (page 93) can be substituted for ground beef, chopped onion and green pepper.

Cook pasta until just barely tender; drain thoroughly and rinse with cold water to stop cooking process. Brown ground beef; drain. Add onion and green pepper to meat and sauté until vegetables are softened (if needed, add small amount of olive oil during sauté process). Add spaghetti sauce. Combine sauce and cooked pasta; mix well. Divide sauce and pasta mixture into three gallon-sized freezer bags; label. Divide grated mozzarella cheese into three quart-sized freezer bags; attach to pasta bags. Freeze.

To Serve:
Thaw. Spread pasta into 9x13-inch baking pan. Sprinkle mozzarella evenly over pasta. Sprinkle ¼ cup Parmesan cheese over top. Cover dish and bake for 30 minutes at 350°, or until bubbly on the edges and hot in the middle. Remove foil and bake five more minutes.

BROCCOLI-HAM BAKE
(12 servings)

4 cups broccoli, cooked and chopped

2 pounds frozen french fries

1 (10¾-ounce) can cream of mushroom soup

1 (10¾-ounce) can cream of broccoli soup

2 cups milk

2-3 cups ham, cubed

2 cups yellow cheese (any variety), grated

Spread frozen french fries in two greased (or sprayed) 9x13-inch baking dishes. Sprinkle chopped broccoli over fries. In a separate bowl, blend soups and milk; stir in ham; pour over fries and broccoli. Wrap baking dish; label and freeze. Place grated cheese in two small freezer bags and attach to baking dish with Broccoli-Ham Bake.

To Serve:

Thaw. Sprinkle grated cheese over top of casserole. Bake at 350° for 25-30 minutes.

HAM AND CHEESE QUICHE
(4-6 servings)

For Crust:
1-2 cups rice (white or brown)
1 egg, beaten
1 teaspoon soy sauce

For Filling:
1-2 cups diced ham
2 sliced green onions
4 eggs, beaten
1½ cups milk, cream or half-and-half
1 cup cheese, grated (use whatever you have available—Swiss, cheddar, Monterey Jack, etc.)
Salt to taste (optional)
¼ teaspoon pepper
Dash nutmeg or ground mace

To Prepare Crust:
Mix together rice, egg and soy sauce. Spread evenly to cover bottom and sides of well buttered quiche pan or pie plate. Bake crust at 350° for 10 minutes. Remove from oven.

To Prepare Filling:
Spread diced ham over bottom of crust. Sprinkle sliced green onions over top of ham. In a bowl, mix together eggs, milk and spices. Pour over ham and green onions. Top with grated cheese. Bake at 350° for 45-50 minutes, or until knife inserted near center of quiche comes out clean. Cool completely. Wrap, label and freeze.

ALL-PURPOSE GROUND MEAT MIX
(Makes about 6 cups)

2½ pound ground meat (beef or turkey)
1 cup celery, chopped
1 clove garlic, minced
1 cup onion, chopped
½ cup green pepper, diced
¼ teaspoon pepper
½ teaspoon salt (optional)

In a large pot, brown ground beef. Drain. Stir in celery, garlic, onion, green pepper, salt and pepper; cover and simmer about 10 minutes, until vegetables are tender but not soft.

EASY TACO SALADS
(6 servings)

2 cups cooked Ground Beef Mixture (page 93)
1 package taco seasonings
water
1 large bag corn chips or tortilla chips
lettuce, shredded
2 cups grated cheese
2 tomatoes, diced
2 green onions, sliced
1 (4-ounce) can black olives (optional)
1 cup sour cream
8 ounces salsa

Add one package taco seasoning to Ground Meat Mixture; cook according to package directions using recommended amount of water from package. On individual plates place a layer of corn chips or tortilla chips; spoon taco mixture over chips. Add a layer of shredded lettuce, grated cheese, diced tomatoes, sliced green onions, sliced black olives, sour cream and salsa to each plate. Serve.

TEXAS-STYLE CHILI
(12 servings)

4 cups Ground Beef Mixture (page 93)

2 tablespoons chili powder

2 tablespoons ground cumin

2 teaspoons salt (optional)

4 (16-ounce) cans crushed tomatoes, undrained

4 (16-ounce) cans red kidney beans, drained (or use home prepared
beans)

3 (16-ounce) cans corn

Place all ingredients into large pot. Bring to a boil. Reduce heat and simmer for at least one hour, stirring occasionally. Cool chili. Put into freezer bags; label and freeze.

To Serve:

Thaw in covered saucepan over low heat. After thawed, increase heat and cook until chili is hot.

TURKEY-STUFFED MANICOTTI
(8 servings)

I've found that cooling the manicotti shells completely before stuffing them makes the stuffing process much easier than attempting to stuff hot noodles. I've also discovered a long handled infant feeding spoon (with a tiny bowl) works perfectly for stuffing manicotti shells.

    2 tablespoons butter, melted
    4 cups cooked turkey meat, chopped or shredded
    2 cups ricotta cheese
    Ground black pepper to taste
    ½ cup Parmesan cheese
    2 green onions, chopped
    1 teaspoon dried parsley
    ½ teaspoon dried rosemary
    2 eggs, lightly beaten
    4 cups tomato sauce, or 2 jars (15-ounce) spaghetti sauce
    16 manicotti shells, cooked until just barely softened

In large skillet, brown turkey in butter for 2-4 minutes. Mix turkey with ricotta cheese. Add pepper, Parmesan, green onions, parsley, rosemary and egg; mix well. Cover bottom of baking pans with one cup tomato sauce. Stuff manicotti shells with turkey mixture; place in baking pan(s) and cover with remaining sauce. Cover baking pan(s) with foil; label and freeze.

<u>To Serve:</u>

Thaw. Sprinkle ½ cup Parmesan cheese over manicotti. Bake uncovered at 350° for 35 minutes, or until bubbly and hot in the center.

TURKEY RICE
(12 servings)

3 cups cooked rice

4 cups cooked turkey, chopped

2 small onions, chopped

1 cup celery, chopped

2 cups yellow cheese, grated

4 (10¾-ounce) cans cream of mushroom soup

salt and pepper to taste

In large bowl, mix together all ingredients. Divide between two 9x13-inch casserole dishes. Cover with foil; label and freeze. Or divide into two labeled freezer bags; freeze.

To Serve:

Thaw. Bake at 350° for 30 minutes, or until bubbly and hot in the center.

HOLIDAY BREAKFAST CASSEROLE
(8 servings)

6-8 slices bread (white or wheat), crusts removed
1 medium apple, peeled and diced
1 pound bulk sausage, cooked (or crumbled links)
2 cups milk (or half-and-half)
1 teaspoon salt
1 teaspoon dry mustard
5 eggs
6 ounces cheddar cheese, shredded

Lay bread in bottom of oblong 9x13-inch glass baking pan. Sprinkle cooked sausage and chopped apple evenly over bread. Sprinkle on cheese. In a bowl, whip together eggs, milk, salt and dry mustard. Pour egg mixture over all; wrap pan well; label and freeze.

To serve:

Thaw completely. Bake in 350 F oven for 35-40 minutes. Let set 10 minutes before serving.

TURKEY NOODLE SOUP
(10 servings)

10 cups turkey broth
>(If necessary add chicken bouillon cubes and water
>to equal 10 cups—dissolve 1 bouillon cube for every 2 cups
>of water)

Any leftover turkey pieces or tidbits

1 cup chopped onion (or however much is leftover from cooking the
>Holiday Meal Plan)

1-2 cups thinly sliced carrots

6 ounces frozen peas

1 teaspoon thyme

1 teaspoon sage

1-2 cloves minced garlic

1 teaspoon oregano

salt and pepper to taste

1 tablespoon parsley

12 ounces egg noodles

Bring stock to boil in large stock pot or Dutch oven. Add all ingredients *except* noodles; reduce heat; simmer one hour. Remove from heat and add noodles. Cool soup completely in refrigerator. Pour into labeled freezer bags; freeze.

8

More Main Dish Dinner Recipes

Don't consider this book to contain an exhaustive list of recipes for establishing your supply of Frozen Assets. These recipes are intended to be samples of what you can use for cooking ahead for the freezer. The following recipes are not necessarily gourmet fare, but they're family favorites that have been tested in the freezer and chosen with the eating habits of real families in mind.

Maybe you'll find some new family favorite recipes in this book. I hope so. These recipes are family-tested, practical, real-world recipes. I've found that most people who seek out a bulk-cooking method are seeking simple and tasty recipes that are affordable while using common ingredients.

Many of these recipes have been adapted from suggestions sent to me via e-mail, and others are family favorites or have been shared by close friends.

Don't be afraid to substitute ingredients or play around with these recipes. Be creative! Rather than changing your eating habits to suit a cooking method, take these meals and this method and suit it to your family's individual tastes and budget. Please feel free to use your own personal recipes or adapt these recipes in any way you desire. Make the recipes lower in fat, or less expensive. Use your imagination. You'll find a list of suggestions for reducing fat in recipes in Appendix D.

You'll find several recipes for large batches of sauce or meat mixtures which you can use in a variety of ways. For example, the spaghetti sauce recipe will have a listing of other uses besides the standard "sauce over pasta" meal.

Happy infrequent cooking!

BULK SPAGHETTI SAUCE
(36 servings)

Ground beef, turkey, pork or any combination of ground meats can be used in this recipe, but the recommended Italian sausage is the tastiest. You can also prepare this without meat, or you can substitute with TVP.

2 pounds Italian sausage
2 cups onions, chopped
½ cup green pepper, chopped
½ cup celery, chopped
2 teaspoons garlic, minced
5 jars commercial spaghetti sauce (or 12 cups homemade sauce)
4 (16-ounce) cans Italian-style stewed tomatoes, cut up, undrained
1 large can sliced black olives

Brown sausage, onion, green pepper, celery and garlic in large Dutch oven or stock pot. Add spaghetti sauce and stewed tomatoes. Simmer on low to medium heat for at least one hour. Stir occasionally. Add black olives after simmering. Allow to cool. Divide into meal-sized portions; pour into labeled freezer bags; freeze.

Suggested uses for spaghetti sauce:
Serve as sauce over pasta.
Use in Lasagna (page 102).
Serve over Meatballs (page 53) with mozzarella cheese on hoagie rolls.
Filling for Calzones (page 137).
Sauce for Chicken Cacciatore (page 122).
Use in Spaghetti Pie (page 104).
Use in Baked Ziti (page 103).

LAZY LASAGNA
(10 servings)

When preparing lasagna for the freezer there's no need to precook the noodles. If you layer the casserole with dry noodles ensuring your noodles are completely covered with sauce, the noodles will cook during the freezing and baking process absorbing the sauce.

12 ounces lasagna noodles, uncooked
½ teaspoon dried oregano
6 cups spaghetti sauce
2 cups cream-style small curd cottage cheese, or ricotta
12 ounces mozzarella cheese, sliced or grated
½ cup grated Parmesan cheese

Stir oregano into spaghetti sauce. In two greased 10x6x2-inch baking dishes, make layers in the following order: half each noodles, cottage cheese, mozzarella slices, spaghetti sauce, and sprinkled Parmesan cheese. Repeat. Make certain the dry noodles are completely covered by sauce. Wrap pans completely with foil; label and freeze.

(To make this meal incredibly rich, add one 8-ounce package cream cheese. Pinch off nickel-sized portions of cream cheese and plop evenly over lasagna just before adding the second layer of uncooked pasta.)

To Serve:

To thaw, take meal from freezer at least 24 hours before serving. Place in refrigerator. Bake tightly covered at 350° for about 45 minutes, or until edges are bubbly and center is hot. Take cover off during final 10 minutes of cooking time. Let stand 10 minutes before serving.

BAKED ZITI
(18 servings)

3 pounds Ziti (or Penne) pasta

1 pound ground beef (optional)

1 cup onion, chopped

1 cup green pepper, chopped

2 jars commercial spaghetti sauce (or 6 cups homemade)

3 cups mozzarella cheese, grated

¾ cup grated Parmesan cheese (to be used at serving time—not during initial prep)

note: Three cups Ground Meat Mixture (see page 66) can be substituted for ground beef, chopped onion and green pepper.

Cook pasta until just barely tender; drain thoroughly and rinse with cold water to stop cooking process. Brown ground beef; drain. Add onion and green pepper to meat and sauté until vegetables are softened (if needed, add small amount of olive oil during sauté process). Add spaghetti sauce. Combine sauce and cooked pasta; mix well. Divide sauce and pasta mixture into three gallon-sized freezer bags; label. Divide grated mozzarella into three quart-sized freezer bags; attach to pasta bags. Freeze.

To Serve:

Thaw. Spread pasta into 9x13-inch baking pan. Sprinkle mozzarella evenly over pasta. Sprinkle ¼ cup Parmesan cheese over top. Cover dish and bake for 30 minutes at 350°, or until bubbly on the edges and hot in the middle. Remove foil and bake five more minutes.

SPAGHETTI PIE
(6 servings)

This recipe can easily be double or tripled. The original Spaghetti Pie recipe calls for a full pound of ground beef, but I only use half a pound per pie. I find half a pound to be more than enough. This recipe could also be made with ground turkey, Italian bulk sausage, TVP or without meat.

6 ounces dry spaghetti noodles
2 tablespoons butter or margarine
½ cup Parmesan cheese
2 well beaten eggs
½ pound ground beef
½ cup chopped onion
1 (8-ounce) can Italian-style stewed tomatoes, undrained
1 (6-ounces) can tomato paste
1 teaspoon sugar
1 teaspoon dried oregano, crushed
½ clove garlic, minced
1 cup cottage cheese
½ cup shredded cheese (your choice: mozzarella, cheddar, American, Montery Jack)

(One cup Ground Meat Mixture can be substituted for ground beef and chopped onion; and 1½ cups bulk spaghetti sauce can be substituted for tomatoes, tomato paste and spices. If using pre-made ingredients, mix the spaghetti sauce and meat mixture together and heat through. Follow all other directions below.)

Cook spaghetti noodles. Drain. Stir margarine into hot noodles until melted. Stir in Parmesan cheese and eggs. Form pasta mixture into a crust-shape in a buttered 9-inch pie plate. In skillet, cook ground beef and onions until meat is browned. Drain. Add tomatoes, tomato paste, sugar, oregano and garlic. Heat through. Spread cottage cheese over bottom of spaghetti crust. Top with tomato and meat mixture. Sprinkle grated cheese over all. Cover pie pan with foil; label and freeze.

To Serve:

Thaw. Bake covered for 25 minutes at 350°. Remove foil and bake for five more minutes or until cheese is lightly browned.

BEEF MIX FOR MEATLOAF AND MEATBALLS
(3 meatloaves and 4 meals of meatballs)

Cooking up a large batch of this meat mixture goes a long way toward establishing a supply of Frozen Assets. From this one recipe, you can make Meatloaf, Meatballs and Salisbury Steak. On the pages following this recipe there are ideas for sauces and other plans for serving meatballs. You can pour the various sauces over sliced meatloaf, too.

24 ounces tomato sauce

3 cups dry bread crumbs

7 eggs, lightly beaten

1 cup onion, finely chopped

½ cup green pepper, finely chopped

2 teaspoons salt, optional

¼ teaspoon dried thyme, crushed

¼ teaspoon dried marjoram, crushed

8 pounds ground beef

Combine first 8 ingredients. Add ground beef and mix well. Divide meat mixture in half.

For Meatloaf:

Shape half the meat mixture into three loaves and place in a large high-sided baking dish. Don't allow the loaves to touch while baking. Bake at 350° for one hour. Cool; wrap in heavy-duty foil; label and freeze. To serve, thaw loaves and bake in 350° oven for 30 minutes or until heated through.

For Meatballs:

Shape into meatballs (use small cookie scoop if available) and place on broiler pan so grease can drain while cooking. Bake uncovered in 350° oven for 30 minutes. Divide into meal-sized portions. To prevent from freezing into a solid meatball-mass, freeze individually on cookie sheets and then place in freezer bags. Label and freeze. To serve, thaw and reheat with your choice of sauces.

For Salisbury Steak:

Form meat mixture into oval ½-inch thick patties. Heat non-stick skillet over medium heat until hot. Place beef patty in skillet; cook seven to eight minutes or until centers are no longer pink, turning once. Cool; place in freezer bags; freeze. Thaw; heat with 1 (10¾-ounce) can cream of mushroom soup poured over as sauce; serve with rice or noodles.

ASSORTED MEATBALL OPTIONS:

The following recipes are various ways to use frozen meatballs. The sauces require some preparation, but the meals go together quickly with your stockpile of precooked meatballs in the freezer.

- Meatball Sandwiches (page 53).
- Sweet-Sour Meatballs (page 109).
- Chili-Day Meatballs (page 110).
- East Indian Meatballs (page 111).
- Tomato-Sauced Meatballs (page 113).
- Meatball Stroganoff (page 114).
- California Meatballs (page 115).
- Heat in brown gravy and serve with mashed potatoes.
- Serve on skewers. (Kids love this!)
- Add to vegetable soup.

SWEET-SOUR MEATBALLS
(5 servings)

1 (14-ounce) can pineapple tidbits or chunks, undrained

¼ cup brown sugar

2 tablespoons cornstarch

½ cup water

¼ cup cider vinegar

1 teaspoon soy sauce (or more to taste)

1 family meal-sized portion of freezer meatballs

1 (5-ounce) can water chestnuts, drained and thinly sliced

1 green pepper, cut in strips

Drain pineapple tidbits, reserving syrup. In medium saucepan, combine brown sugar and cornstarch. Blend in reserved syrup, water, cider vinegar and soy sauce. Cook and stir over low heat until thick and bubbly. Carefully stir in meatballs, water chestnuts, green pepper strips, and pineapple. Heat to boiling. Serve over hot cooked rice.

CHILI-DAY MEATBALLS
(5 servings)

1 (12-ounce) jar chili sauce (or 1½ cups homemade)

11-ounce jar grape jelly

2 tablespoons lemon juice

1 cube beef bouillon dissolved in ½ cup water

1 family meal-sized portion of freezer meatballs

Whisk together chili sauce, grape jelly, lemon juice and bouillon breaking up all clumps. Simmer on low heat until sauce starts to thicken. Add freezer meatballs; cook in sauce until meatballs are fully thawed and heated through. Serve over cooked noodles or rice.

Crockpot Method:

Mix together sauce as described above. Place frozen meatballs in crockpot, pouring sauce over them. Stir gently to coat. Cook for eight hours on a low setting.

EAST-INDIAN MEATBALLS
(5 servings)

1 tablespoon butter
1 cup pared apple, finely chopped
1 clove garlic, minced
1 cup sliced celery
½ cup onion, chopped
2 tablespoons cornstarch
2 teaspoons curry powder
2 teaspoons sugar
1 cup beef broth
1 (3-ounce) can sliced mushrooms (or ½ cup fresh, sautéed in butter until soft)
1 family meal-sized portion of freezer meatballs

In saucepan, melt butter; add apple, garlic, celery and onion. Cook until onion is tender. Combine cornstarch, curry, sugar and beef broth. Stir into onion mixture. Simmer, stirring until mixture thickens and bubbles. Stir in meatballs and mushrooms. Simmer until meatballs are heated through. Serve over hot cooked rice or in East Indian Rice Ring (recipe on page 111).

EAST-INDIAN RICE RING
(Serve with East-Indian Meatballs* or Chicken Curry*)

¼ cup butter
½ cup onion, chopped
¼ cup slivered almonds
½ cup light raisins
6 cups hot cooked rice
Shredded coconut (optional)

In skillet, melt butter and sauté chopped onion and almonds until golden. Add light raisins; heat until plump. Add hot rice; mix gently. Press mixture into greased 6½ cup ring mold. Remove from mold at once and place on to a round serving platter. Fill center of rice ring with East Indian Meatballs (page 110) or Chicken Curry (page 127). If desired, top with a sprinkling of shredded coconut.

TOMATO-SAUCED MEATBALLS
(5 servings)

1 (10¾-ounce) can condensed tomato soup
½ cup water
1 teaspoon Worcestershire sauce
1 family meal-sized portion of freezer meatballs

Mix together: soup, water and Worcestershire sauce. Place meatballs in a medium sized saucepan; pour soup mixture over meatballs. Simmer until meatballs are heated through. Serve over hot cooked rice.

MEATBALL STROGANOFF
(5 servings)

1 (10 ¾-ounce) can condensed cream of mushroom soup
½ cup sour cream, or plain yogurt
1 cup mushrooms (optional), sliced and cooked in butter until soft
1 family meal-sized portion of freezer meatballs

In medium saucepan, mix together mushroom soup and sour cream (or yogurt). Gently stir in mushrooms (if used), and meatballs. Simmer until meatballs are heated through. Serve over hot cooked rice, or over egg noodles tossed with melted butter and parsley.

CALIFORNIA MEATBALLS
(5 servings)

1 medium onion, thinly sliced (optional)
2 teaspoons olive oil
1 bottle Catalina salad dressing
1 family meal-sized portion of freezer meatballs

Sauté onion slices in olive oil until softened. Place frozen meatballs in medium skillet. Pour dressing over meatballs. Cover skillet and cook over low heat until dressing caramelizes on meatballs and onion, and the meatballs are fully thawed and heated through. Serve over rice.

ALL-PURPOSE GROUND MEAT MIX
(Makes about 12 cups)

This is a basic ground meat mix that can be used in many casseroles that require a meat mixture. Several recipes for using this mix are on the pages that follow.

> 5 pounds ground meat (beef or turkey)
> 2 cups celery, chopped
> 1 clove garlic, minced
> 2 cups onion, chopped
> 1 cup green pepper, diced
> ½ teaspoon pepper
> 1 teaspoon salt (optional)

In a large pot, brown ground beef. Drain. Stir in celery, garlic, onion, green pepper, salt and pepper; cover and simmer about 10 minutes, until vegetables are tender but not soft. You can use this mixture immediately during your cooking session or freeze in two cup portions for later use.

SUGGESTED USES (be creative):

Tacos: add 1 package taco seasoning to two cups All-Purpose Ground Meat Mix (follow package directions for amount of water). Freeze. To serve: thaw and heat taco mixture; prepare tacos as you would normally.

Taco Potatoes: follow instructions for taco mixture (above), but serve the mixture over baked potatoes instead of tortillas or taco shells. Top with grated cheese, diced tomatoes, sour cream, sliced green onions, sliced black olives and salsa.

Easy Taco Salads: follow instructions for taco mixture; place a layer of corn chips or tortilla chips on plate; spoon taco mixture over chips; add layer of shredded lettuce; add diced tomatoes, sliced green onions, sliced black olives, sour cream and salsa.

The All-Purpose Ground Meat Mix can also be used for:

Stuffed Peppers	(see page 118)
Sloppy Joes	(see page 119)
Texas Chili	(see page 120)
Spaghetti Pie	(see page 104)
Baked Ziti	(see page 103)

STUFFED PEPPERS
(12 servings)

12 large green peppers
2 cups All-Purpose Ground Meat Mix (or brown together 1 pound
    ground beef, 2 cups chopped onion and 2 cloves minced garlic)
2 teaspoon paprika
2 cups cooked rice (long-grain is best but use what you have)
24 ounces tomato sauce
2 (10¾-ounce) cans tomato soup (save until serving day)

Cut off tops of green peppers; remove seeds. Mix together All-Purpose Ground Meat Mix, rice, spices and tomato sauce. Stuff meat and rice mixture into green peppers. Place in roasting pan. Bake covered at 350° for 40 minutes. Cool. Wrap individually in foil; label and freeze.

To Serve:

Unwrap stuffed peppers. Place in roasting pan. Pour tomato soup over peppers. Heat at 350 for 25 minutes. Or unwrap and cook in microwave oven.

SLOPPY JOES
(4-6 servings)

This is a simple recipe that is easy to double or triple. My family loves sloppy joes. (Must be something about the fact that for once it's okay to be messy while eating.)

2 cups All-Purpose Ground Meat Mix (or brown together 1 pound ground beef and 1 small onion, chopped)
1 (10¾-ounce) can tomato soup
2 tablespoons brown sugar
1 teaspoon prepared mustard

Place Ground Meat Mix into large skillet. Add tomato soup, brown sugar and mustard; stir. Cover and simmer 10 minutes. Freeze.

To Serve:

Thaw and heat Sloppy Joe mix in skillet. Serve ladled on to hamburger buns.

TEXAS-STYLE CHILI
(12 servings)

4 cups All-Purpose Ground Meat Mix
2 tablespoons chili powder
2 tablespoons ground cumin
2 teaspoons salt (optional)
4 (16-ounce) cans crushed tomatoes, undrained
4 (16-ounce) cans red kidney beans, drained (or use home prepared
   beans)
3 cans corn

Place all ingredients into large pot. Bring to a boil. Reduce heat and simmer for at least one hour, stirring occasionally. Cool chili. Put into freezer bags; label and freeze.

<u>To Serve:</u>
Thaw in covered saucepan over low heat. After thawed, increase heat and cook until chili is hot.

POOR MAN'S CASSEROLE
(6 servings)

2 cups Ground Beef Mixture (page 66)
1 pound frozen vegetables (your choice, any combination)
Spices (whatever you like: marjoram, parsley, Italian spice, ground pepper, etc.)
3 cups mashed potatoes
1 cup yellow cheese, grated

Mix meat with vegetables and place in 9x13-inch casserole dish. Add spices. Spread mashed potatoes over top of meat and vegetable mixture. Sprinkle grated cheese over top of potatoes. Wrap casserole in foil; label and freeze.

To Serve:
Thaw. Heat uncovered in 350° oven for 20-30 minutes, or until heated through.

MEXI-CHICKEN
(18 servings)

2 cups onion, chopped

2 cloves garlic (or more to taste), minced

2 tablespoons vegetable oil

4 cups water

2 cups Quaker Quick barley (regular barley can be used, but cooking
   time increases dramatically)

2 (16-ounce) cans chopped tomatoes, undrained

2 (16-ounce) cans tomato sauce

3 cups chicken broth

2 (16-ounce) cans whole kernel corn, drained

6 cups cooked chicken, chopped or shredded

Spices:

Either use 2 tablespoons chili powder and 1 teaspoon cumin *or* use two packages of taco seasonings

In large Dutch oven, cook onion and garlic in oil until tender. Add all ingredients except chicken. Bring to boil. Reduce heat and simmer 10 minutes, stirring occasionally. Add cooked chicken; continue simmering for another 10 minutes, or until chicken is heated through and barley is tender. Cool; spoon into freezer bags; label and freeze.

If you're using regular barley, rather than the quick cooking variety, you'll need to cook the barley ahead of time. Allow one hour for barley to cook. Follow directions on barley.

To Serve:

Thaw chicken mixture. Heat in skillet until hot. Serve over corn tortilla chips or scoop into flour tortillas fajita-style.

CHICKEN CACCIATORE
(15 servings)

This recipe can also be made with whole chicken pieces. Bake the individual chicken pieces before freezing. Prepare the sauce (minus chicken). Pour the sauce into freezer bags; add cooked chicken pieces. Label and freeze. To serve: thaw and heat in skillet until chicken pieces are heated through.

3 cups chicken, cooked and cubed
1 tablespoon olive oil
2 medium onions, sliced thinly
1 green pepper, sliced thinly
1½ cups mushrooms, sliced
2 cloves garlic, minced (or 2 teaspoons)
6 cups homemade spaghetti sauce (or two 15-ounce jars of commercial sauce plus one can Italian-style stewed tomatoes)

In large skillet or Dutch oven, sauté onion, green pepper, mushrooms and garlic until onion is soft. Stir in chicken and spaghetti sauce. Simmer 15 minutes. Allow to cool. Package in freezer bags. Label and freeze.

To Serve:
Thaw. Pour into medium saucepan; simmer until heated through. Serve over wide egg noodles, spaghetti or rice. Sprinkle with Parmesan cheese if desired.

CHICKEN CASSEROLE
(12 servings)

5 cups cooked chicken, diced
5 cups celery, chopped
1 bunch green onions, sliced with tops
1 (5¾-ounce) can sliced olives
1 cup slivered almonds
2 cups cheddar cheese, grated
1 cup mayonnaise (use salad dressing when preparing for freezing)
1 cup sour cream
2 cups crushed potato chips (not needed until serving day)

In large bowl, combine chicken, celery, green onions, olives and almonds. Add 1 cup cheese. In separate bowl, mix mayonnaise and sour cream; combine mayonnaise (or salad dressing) mixture with chicken mixture. Spoon into two greased 8x8-inch baking pans. Cover with foil; label. Place remaining cheese into a small freezer bag; label; attach to casserole dish. Freeze casserole and cheese bag together.

To Serve:
Thaw casserole and bag of cheese. Sprinkle crushed potato chips over top of casserole; top with remaining cheese. Bake uncovered at 350° for 25 minutes, or until hot.

SOUTH OF THE BORDER CHICKEN BAKE
(18 servings)

2 (10¾-ounce) cans cream of mushroom soup
2 (10¾-ounce) cans cream of chicken soup
3½ cups milk
4 cups cooked chicken, chopped
2 onions, finely chopped
2 cups salsa
4 cups cheddar cheese, grated
24 corn tortillas, each cut into 8 pieces

In large bowl, combine soups and milk; stir well. Add chicken, onion, salsa and three cups of grated cheese. Layer tortilla pieces first followed by chicken mixture into three lightly buttered 8x8-inch baking pans. Top with remaining cheese. Cover with foil; label and freeze.

To Serve:
Thaw casserole. Bake in 350° oven for 35-45 minutes, or until bubbly.

CHICKEN BROCCOLI
(16 servings)

1 cup margarine
1 cup flour
8 cups milk
Salt and pepper to taste
4 cups cooked chicken, chopped
2 pounds broccoli, steamed
2 pounds cheddar cheese, grated

<u>Make white sauce</u>: melt margarine in a large heavy pan. Add flour, stirring constantly. When it reaches the boiling point, add milk, mixing constantly with a wire whisk. Heat until almost boiling, stirring constantly. Remove from heat. Place cooked chicken into four 8x8-inch baking pans. Divide steamed broccoli and place over chicken. Pour white sauce over all. Sprinkle each pan with grated cheese. Cover pans with foil; label and freeze. This recipe can also be frozen in zip-top freezer bags to conserve space in your freezer. If storing in bags, divide grated cheese among smaller freezer bags and freeze separately from the chicken and broccoli.

<u>To Serve:</u>
Thaw. Bake at 350° for 30 minutes. Serve over cooked rice or spaghetti noodles for a Tetrazinni-type meal.

CHICKEN CREOLE
(20 servings)

4 tablespoons butter
2 cups onion, chopped
2 cups celery, chopped
1 (6-ounce) can tomato paste
½ cup water
2 (16-ounce) can tomatoes, diced
3 tablespoons Worcestershire sauce
1 tablespoon chili powder
1 teaspoon salt
2 teaspoon sugar
Tabasco sauce, to taste
¼ teaspoon unflavored gelatin, dissolved in 2 tablespoons cold water
5 cups cooked chicken, diced (or 2 pounds shrimp, cooked)

Sauté onions and celery in butter until tender. In separate bowl, stir together tomato paste and water until smooth. Add tomato paste and water to saucepan. Stir in tomatoes, Worcestershire sauce, salt, sugar, chili powder and Tabasco. Simmer uncovered for 40 minutes. Stir in dissolved gelatin. Remove from heat; cool. Stir in chicken pieces and divide into freezer bags.

To Serve:

Thaw and heat in saucepan until warmed through. Serve with hot cooked rice.

CHICKEN CURRY
(10 servings)

2 tablespoons butter
2 cups pared apple, finely chopped
2 cups celery, sliced
1 cup onion, chopped
2 cloves garlic, minced
4 tablespoons cornstarch
4-6 teaspoons curry powder (to taste)
1 teaspoon salt (optional)
1½ cups cold chicken broth
4 cups milk
4 cups cooked chicken, diced
2 (3-ounce) cans sliced mushrooms, drained (or 1 cup sliced fresh)

In saucepan, melt butter; add apple, celery, onion and garlic. Cook until onion is tender. In separate bowl, combine cornstarch, curry, salt and broth. Stir into onion and apple mixture; add milk. Cook and stir until mixture thickens and bubbles. Stir in chicken and mushrooms. Heat through. Divide into freezer bags; label and freeze.

To Serve:
Thaw. In saucepan, heat thoroughly. Serve Chicken Curry over hot cooked rice and pass condiments—raisins, shredded coconut, chopped peanuts, chutney; or serve in East-Indian Rice Ring (page 76).

TURKEY-STUFFED MANICOTTI
(8 servings)

This is a wonderful way to use up leftover Thanksgiving turkey.

2 tablespoons butter
4 cups cooked turkey meat, chopped or shredded
2 cups ricotta cheese
Ground black pepper to taste
½ cup Parmesan cheese
2 green onions, chopped
1 teaspoon dried parsley
½ teaspoon dried rosemary
2 eggs, lightly beaten
4 cups tomato sauce
16 manicotti shells, cooked until just barely softened

In large skillet, brown turkey for 2-4 minutes. Mix turkey with Ricotta. Add pepper, Parmesan, green onions, parsley, rosemary and egg; mix well. Cover bottom of baking pans with 1 cup of the tomato sauce. Stuff manicotti shells with turkey mixture; place in baking pans and cover with remaining sauce. Cover baking pans with foil; label and freeze.

<u>To Serve:</u>
Thaw. Sprinkle ½ cup Parmesan cheese over manicotti. Bake uncovered at 350° for 35 minutes, or until hot and bubbly.

TURKEY RICE
(12 servings)

3 cups cooked rice
4 cups cooked turkey, chopped
2 small onions, chopped
1 cup celery, chopped
2 cups yellow cheese, grated
4 (10¾-ounce) cans cream of mushroom soup
salt and pepper to taste

In large bowl, mix together all ingredients. Divide between two 9x13-inch casserole dishes. Cover with foil; label and freeze.

<u>To Serve:</u>
Thaw. Bake at 350° for 30 minutes, or until bubbly and hot in the center.

CRAB AND SWISS QUICHE
(6 servings)

This recipe freezes well and can easily be doubled or tripled. My quiche recipes usually call for a rice crust. I've found that pastry crusts sometimes get soggy when frozen but I've never had that problem with rice crust. Feel free to substitute a pastry shell for the rice crust if you desire. This recipe can be made with either canned crab or imitation crab meat. I've received just as many compliments when I use the imitation crab. You could also substitute cooked shrimp for the crab meat.

Crust:
  2 cups rice, cooked (white or brown)
  1 egg, beaten
  1 teaspoon soy sauce

Filling:
  4 ounces Swiss cheese, grated
  7.5 ounces can crab meat, drained and flaked (or 8 ounces imitation crab meat)
  2 green onions, sliced with tops
  4 eggs, beaten
  1½ cups light cream, or milk (I usually use 2%)
  ½ teaspoon salt (optional)
  ½ teaspoon lemon peel, grated
  ¼ teaspoon dry mustard
  Dash nutmeg or ground mace
  1/8 cup sliced almonds

Crust:

Mix together cooked rice, egg and soy sauce. Spread evenly to cover well-buttered quiche pan or pie plate. Bake rice crust at 350° for 10 minutes. Remove from oven.

Filling:

Arrange cheese on bottom of rice crust. Top with crab meat. Sprinkle with green onions. Mix together: eggs, milk, salt, lemon peel, mustard and nutmeg. Pour evenly over top of quiche. Sprinkle almonds over top. Bake at 350 F for 45 minutes, or until set. Remove from oven and let sit 10 minutes before slicing, if serving fresh; or wrap pie pan, label and freeze. Cooked quiche can be served cold after thawing for a yummy hot weather treat; or heat the thawed quiche at 350° for 25 minutes.

BASIC "USE-IT-UP" QUICHE
(6 servings)

You can use almost any leftover vegetable or meat in this recipe. If you have eggs, milk, rice and cheese, you can practically clean out your refrigerator right into your quiche pan. I always add the cheese last when making this quiche. The cheese makes a beautiful mellow-brown crust on the top. I usually add a bit of chopped onion to my quiches for flavor. Broccoli makes an especially nice vegetable quiche.

Crust:
  2 cups rice, cooked (white or brown)
  1 egg, beaten
  1 teaspoon soy sauce

Filling:
  ½ pound any leftover vegetable, chopped (single vegetable or a mix)
  4 eggs, beaten
  1½ cups milk or light cream
  1 cup cheese, grated (your choice of Swiss, cheddar, etc.)
  ½ teaspoon salt (optional)
  1/8 teaspoon pepper
  Dash nutmeg or ground mace

Crust:
Mix together cooked rice, egg and soy sauce. Spread evenly to cover well-buttered quiche pan or pie plate. Bake rice crust at 350° for 10 minutes. Remove from oven.

Filling:
Place chopped vegetable in bottom of crust. Mix together: eggs, milk, salt, pepper and nutmeg. Pour over broccoli. Top with grated cheese. Bake

at 350° for 45 minutes, or until set. Remove from oven, and let set ten minutes before slicing, if serving fresh; or wrap pie pan, label and freeze. Quiche can be served cold after thawing; or heat the thawed quiche at 350° for 20 minutes.

SUGGESTED QUICHE COMBINATIONS

Quiche Lorraine—cooked and crumbled bacon with Swiss cheese.

Chicken Elegante—1 pound cooked chicken, chopped; ½ cup green
    pepper; ½ cup   sliced mushrooms.

Spinach—spread 1 pound finely chopped, well-drained cooked spinach
    over Swiss cheese.

Quiche Nicoise—one medium, thinly sliced tomato; 1/3 cup sliced ripe
    olives; add ¼ teaspoon garlic powder with other spices (leaving out
    nutmeg).

Green Chile and Cheese Pie—1½ cups Monterey Jack cheese; 1
    (4-ounce) can chopped green chilies; 1/8 teaspoon cumin for spice
    (no nutmeg).

CRUSTLESS "USE-IT-UP" QUICHE
(6 servings)

No pie shell or rice crust is needed. The biscuit mix makes its own crust.

1½ cups milk
½ cup biscuit mix (i.e. Bisquick)
3 eggs, lightly beaten
¼ teaspoon salt (optional)
1/8 teaspoon pepper
Dash of nutmeg or ground mace
½ to 1 cup any cooked vegetable, chopped
¾ cup cheese (most any variety), grated
1/3 cup onion, chopped

Lightly grease pie pan or quiche dish. Beat milk, biscuit mix, eggs, salt, pepper and nutmeg until smooth, and pour into pan. Sprinkle vegetables and cheese over egg mixture. Bake at 400° for 30 minutes until golden brown and knife inserted near center comes out clean. Let stand 10 minutes before serving, if serving fresh; or wrap pie pan, label and freeze. Quiche can be served cold after thawing; or heat the thawed quiche at 350° for 20 minutes.

STUFFED POTATO SHELLS
(12 main dish servings; or 24 side dish servings)

12 baking potatoes, scrubbed

1 teaspoon salt (optional)

¼ teaspoon pepper (or more to taste)

¼ cup margarine, or butter

  (small amount of milk may be needed during preparation)

½ cup onion, chopped

1½ cups cheddar cheese, grated

1½ cups Monterey Jack cheese, grated

2 boxes frozen, chopped spinach, thawed and drained

Bake potatoes at 400 F for 1 hour. Remove from oven. Slice hot potatoes in half lengthwise. Carefully scoop out pulp into large bowl, leaving a thin potato-skin shell. Mash potato pulp with salt, pepper and margarine (and milk, if needed). Stir in chopped onion, both cheeses, and spinach. Heap potato, spinach and cheese mixture into potato shells.

To Serve Immediately:

Bake the filled potato shells at 400° for 20 minutes, or until golden brown.

To Freeze:

Fill potato shells with spinach mixture, but don't reheat stuffed potato shells in oven. Freeze potatoes by placing them on a cookie sheet in the freezer for a few minutes until hard. Pack the hardened potato shells into heavy-duty freezer bags.

To Serve:

Remove from bag (as many as needed). Allow to thaw; place on cookie sheet, or in shallow baking dish. Bake at 400° for 20 minutes, or until golden brown.

CALZONES
(12 servings)

These are little dough-wrapped baked sandwiches. This recipe for calzone dough can be filled with practically anything: a small amount of spaghetti sauce (a tad too much sauce makes them drippy beyond belief so use sparingly) and mozzarella cheese; spinach; broccoli. Take a look at some of the dough-wrapped freezer sandwiches in the grocery freezer section for more ideas of what to put into these sandwiches. You can also make simple calzones using frozen bread dough from the store.

    2 tablespoons yeast
    2 cups warm water (but not hot)
    5 cups flour
    2 cups corn meal
    2 tablespoons salt
    5 tablespoons olive oil

Dissolve yeast in warm water until foamy. Stir in flour, corn meal, sugar, salt and olive oil. Let rise one hour. Divide into 12 equal balls. Flatten dough balls into 12 8-inch rounds. Put filling on to rounds and fold in half. Pinch edges to seal. Prick tops several times with fork. Sprinkle corn meal on to cookie sheet. Bake calzones at 425 F for 18-20 minutes. Cool, wrap individually and freeze.

To Serve:
Thaw. Reheat in oven until hot, or microwave.

Suggested Filling Ideas:
Spaghetti sauce and mozarella cheese
Spaghetti sauce and pepperoni slices
Sliced ham with Swiss or Havarti cheese
Chopped cooked chicken, cream cheese and chives
Chopped cooked chicken and cooked broccoli pieces

PIZZA BLANKS

(2 medium size or 4 small pizza blanks)

Submitted by Gina Dalquest

Pre-made Pizza crusts are one of the fastest selling items at grocery stores. Unfortunately, they are also very expensive. With a little effort you can make your own and keep a bunch in your freezer for quick dinners or easy snacks.

Pinch of sugar

1 ¼ cups warm milk

2 packages active dry yeast (I use five teaspoons, because I buy yeast in big bags)

3 1/3 cups flour

½ teaspoon salt

1 egg

Stir sugar into warm milk and sprinkle with yeast. Let stand for five minutes or until frothy. Stir gently to moisten any dry particles. Sift flour and salt into large bowl. Lightly beat egg into yeast mixture, pour into flour mixture, combining to make a dough. On a floured surface knead dough until smooth and springy, 5 to 10 minutes. Cover and let rise in a warm place for 25 minutes. Divide the dough according to your needs and freezer space. Shape each piece into a ball and, on a floured surface, roll to about ½ inch thickness. Place on baking sheets and freeze for one hour. Remove from baking sheets, wrap well in plastic wrap or freezer bags, and place back in freezer. Pizza blanks will keep in the freezer for about a month.

To serve:

Simply thaw, top, and bake at 425 for about 20 minutes or until the cheese is melted and just browning.

BROCCOLI-HAM BAKE
(12 servings)

4 cups broccoli, cooked and chopped

2 pound frozen french fries

1 (10¾-ounce) can cream of mushroom soup

1 (10¾-ounce) can cream of broccoli soup

2 cups milk

2-3 cups ham, cubed

2 cups yellow cheese (any variety), grated

Spread frozen french fries in two greased 9x13-inch baking dishes. Sprinkle chopped broccoli over fries. In a separate bowl, blend soups and milk; stir in ham; pour over fries and broccoli. Wrap baking dish; label and freeze. Place grated cheese in two small freezer bags and attach to baking dish with Broccoli-Ham Bake.

To Serve:

Thaw. Sprinkle grated cheese over top of casserole. Bake at 350° for 25-30 minutes.

SCALLOPED POTATOES AND HAM
(20 servings)

The potatoes will start to turn brown if you don't get them right into the bags with the sauce, so move quickly when preparing this meal.

1 pound ham, in small cubes
5 pounds potatoes, sliced with skin on
1 large onion, chopped
1 pound yellow cheese (any variety), grated
½ cup margarine
½ cup flour
4 cups milk
Salt and pepper to taste

For sauce: melt margarine in heavy pan. Add flour, stirring constantly. Heat to boiling point; add milk; mix constantly with wire whisk. Heat until thickened, stirring constantly. Add spices. In separate pan, sauté meat with onions. Boil sliced potatoes, but remove from heat while still firm. Divide potatoes between five freezer bags. Divide ham and onion mixture, and add to potatoes in freezer bags. Divide white sauce and pour over meat and potatoes in freezer bags. Label and freeze quickly. Divide grated cheese between smaller freezer bags, attatch and freeze.

To Serve:
Thaw potato mixture. Pour into baking pan. Sprinkle with grated cheese. Bake at 350° for 20 minutes, or until heated through.

SPLIT PEA SOUP WITH HAM
(8 servings)

10 cups water
4 cups split peas
1 cup ham, diced
1 teaspoon salt
½ teaspoon pepper
¼ teaspoon marjoram, crushed
1 bay leaf, finely crushed
1 cup celery, chopped
1 cup onion, chopped
1 cup carrots, sliced

Rinse peas; combine peas, water, ham, salt, pepper and marjoram in large Dutch oven or stock pot. Bring to a boil; cover, reduce heat, simmer (don't boil) for 1 ½ hours. Stir occasionally. Add celery, onion and carrots. Simmer, uncovered for 30 minutes.

note: I often substitute Keilbasa for the ham in this recipe.

LENTIL-RICE SOUP
(8 servings)

1 (12-ounce) can tomato paste
2 (16-ounce) cans tomatoes, undrained
8 cups water
2 cups uncooked lentils
2 cups uncooked rice
2 medium onions, chopped
1 cup celery, chopped
2 cloves garlic, minced
Salt and pepper to taste

Put tomato paste and canned tomatoes into large Dutch oven or stock pot. Add water. Stir in all other ingredients. Heat to boiling. Turn down heat and simmer for 1 hour, or until lentils are soft and rice is cooked.

LENTIL RANCHERO
(12 servings)

8 cups cooked lentils

1 pound ground beef   (optional)

2 packages onion soup mix

2 cups catsup

2 teaspoons prepared mustard

2 teaspoons vinegar

2 cups water

In large skillet brown ground beef; drain. Stir in remaining ingredients. Pour into two casserole dishes; bake at 400° for 30 minutes. Cool; wrap casseroles; label and freeze.

To Serve:

Thaw and reheat at 350° for 20 minutes, or until heated through.

BLACK BEANS AND RICE
(8 servings)

2 cans black beans, drained (or use cooked dry beans)
20 ounces frozen corn
2 cups long grain rice, uncooked (white or brown)
32 ounces salsa (your choice: mild, medium or hot)
3 cups tomato juice
½ teaspoon cumin
½ teaspoon oregano
2 cups cheddar cheese, grated

In large bowl, combine all ingredients (except cheese). Pour into two casserole dishes; bake covered at 375° for one hour. Remove from oven. Cool; wrap, label and freeze. Divide grated cheese into two small freezer bags and attach to Black Beans and Rice in freezer.

<u>To Serve:</u>
Thaw. Sprinkle grated cheese over beans and rice; reheat at 350° for 15-20 minutes until cheese is melted and beans and rice are heated through.

MEXICAN NOODLE BAKE
(12 servings)

This recipe can be made with cooked dry beans instead of canned black and kidney beans. Also, zucchini can be added (it's really good this way!), but I would recommend not precooking the zucchini since it becomes mushy in the freezer. Just slice a medium zucchini and stir into the bean and noodle mixture just before wrapping for the freezer.

> 2 cups onion, chopped
> 2 cups bell pepper, chopped
> 2 cups celery, sliced
> 2 packages taco seasoning
> 2 (15-ounce) cans black beans, drained
> 2 (15-ounce) cans red kidney beans, undrained
> 32 ounces tomato sauce
> 32 ounces diced tomatoes, canned
> 4 cups macaroni, cooked until just tender and drained
> 4 cups Cheddar cheese, grated

In large skillet or Dutch oven, lightly sauté onions, green pepper and celery in small amount of butter or margarine until just tender. Stir in taco seasoning packets, both types of beans, tomato sauce and canned tomatoes. Simmer for 10 minutes. Stir in cooked noodles. Spread bean and noodle mixture into two 9x13-inch casserole dishes. Wrap casseroles; label and freeze. Divide grated cheese between two small freezer bags. Attach to casseroles in freezer.

To Serve:

Thaw. Sprinkle grated cheese over top of casserole. Bake uncovered at 375° for 45 minutes, or until center is hot and edges are bubbly.

BEEF AND BEAN BURRITOS
(24 servings)

Submitted by Lynn Nelson

4 tablespoons oil

2 onions, chopped

4 pounds ground beef

4 cloves garlic, minced

2 tablespoons Chili powder

2 teaspoons cumin

Salt and pepper to taste

16 ounces tomato sauce

62 ounces refried beans (canned or homemade)

24 flour tortillas

Sauté onion in oil until tender. Add beef and garlic; cook until beef is no longer pink. Drain. Add chili powder, cumin and other seasonings. Stir in tomato sauce and simmer five minutes. Add refried beans; cook and stir until well blended. Set aside to cool completely. Soften tortillas, if necessary, and place small portion of meat and bean mixture on to center of each. Roll up, burrito-style. These may be frozen as follows: place seam side down on a cookie sheet and freeze until frozen. Wrap each individually and return to freezer.

<u>To Serve:</u>

You can thaw these first and then heat, or just place frozen burrito in microwave until heated through.

ENCHILADA PIE
(15 servings)

This is so good! I could eat it every night, but I think the rest of my family would get a little tired of it after awhile. Prepared according to instructions, this recipe makes a little layered "cake," but naming this recipe Enchilada Cake might be odd—I can almost hear people wondering what sort of frosting or icing to prepare for the cake. For easier and faster preparation, cut the tortillas into one inch pieces and just throw the whole mess into a casserole dish. Tastes the same; it's just not quite as pretty.

  3 pounds ground beef
  3 onions, chopped
  3 teaspoons salt (optional)
  1 teaspoon pepper
  3 tablespoons chili powder
  24 ounces tomato sauce
  18 corn tortillas, spread with butter
  12 ounces black olives, drained and chopped
  3 cups sharp cheddar cheese, shredded
  1½ cups water

Brown ground beef and onion; add seasonings and tomato sauce. In three 2-quart casserole dishes alternate layers of tortillas (tortillas can be cut to fit baking pan), meat sauce, olives and cheese. Add ½ cup water to each casserole. Cover tightly. Label and freeze.

To Serve:
Thaw casserole completely. Bake in 400° oven for 20 minutes.

9

Breakfasts, Lunches, Desserts, Mixes

In many families, morning is a hectic and hurried time. Frequently parents feel fortunate just to get everyone out the door fully dressed each day. Serve a hot breakfast every morning? Not a chance. Breakfast (if it's served at all) often consists of grabbing a toaster pastry and a quick glass of juice as the family runs out the door racing headlong to work and school. Taking an hour or so on a weekend to prepare breakfast items for the freezer can take much of the insanity out of the weekday morning rush.

Likewise, many lunch items and desserts can be prepared for freezing. Sandwiches, slices of quiche and pieces of cake can be placed directly into a lunch box fully frozen, and be thawed for eating by noon, keeping other items cold, too.

At the end of this section I've included a recipe for a Multi-Purpose Baking Mix (much like the boxed biscuit mixes at the grocery store). This mix can be used for preparing the recipes included after it: pancakes, waffles, biscuits, shortcake, snack cake, dumplings and pizza crust.

Breakfasts

Breakfast is an easy meal to prepare for the freezer: sausage and egg casseroles; egg sandwiches, breakfast burritos, pancakes, French toast, waffles, muffins, quick bread, baked oatmeal. Having homemade breakfast items stashed away in your freezer cuts down on that early morning rush, plus the meals are healthier and less expensive than stocking up on similar items from the grocery freezer case.

Many of these items can be reheated quickly in the microwave.

I've included simple recipes for waffles and pancakes in the Multi-Purpose Baking Mix section later in this chapter. To prepare waffles, pancakes and French toast for freezing, cook until lightly browned—don't overcook. For reheating, just pop them into the toaster as you would the boxed frozen waffles from the store (heating in the toaster keeps them firm, rather than limp and soggy which often happens when reheated in the microwave).

HOLIDAY BREAKFAST CASSEROLE
(8 servings)

6-8 slices bread (white or wheat), crusts removed
1 medium apple, peeled and diced
1 pound bulk sausage, cooked (or crumbled links)
2 cups milk (or half-and-half)
1 teaspoon salt
1 teaspoon dry mustard
5 eggs
6 ounces cheddar cheese, shredded

Lay bread in bottom of oblong 9x13-inch glass baking pan. Sprinkle cooked sausage over bread. Sprinkle on cheese. In a bowl, whip together eggs, milk, salt and dry mustard. Pour egg mixture over all and refrigerate overnight (for breakfast) or all day (for dinner). If freezing, skip the refrigeration instructions; wrap pan well; label and freeze.

To serve:
Thaw completely. Bake in 350° oven for 35-40 minutes. Let set 10 minutes before serving.

BREAKFAST SANDWICHES
(2 dozen breakfast sandwiches)

24 English muffins, toasted and buttered
2 dozen eggs
24 regular bacon strips, cooked and drained
24 thin slices cheddar cheese

Scramble eggs in large skillet or fry eggs individually on griddle*. Put sandwiches together (one English muffin, one egg, one strip of bacon cut in half, one slice of cheese). Wrap each sandwich individually in a paper towel, then place several sandwiches in large zip-top freezer bags.

To serve: microwave on high for one to two minutes. Or thaw sandwiches, re-wrap in foil and bake at 400° for 15-20 minutes.

Substitutions:
Fat-free egg substitute can be substituted for eggs.
Large biscuits (homemade or store bought) can be used in place of English muffins. Be sure to undercook biscuits slightly or they'll be too crumbly.
Canadian bacon (back bacon), ham slices or cooked sausage patties can be substituted for regular bacon slices.

note: Cook eggs inside greased canning rings to maintain a round shape.

BREAKFAST BURRITOS
(24 burritos)

12 eggs, beaten
1 pound bulk sausage, cooked (or crumbled links)
½ cup chunky salsa (your choice: mild, medium or hot.)
2 cups cheddar cheese, shredded
24 flour tortillas

Scramble eggs in large skillet until done; stir in cooked sausage and salsa. Warm tortillas in microwave 20-30 seconds or until warm and flexible. Place ½ cup egg mixture into tortilla; roll burrito-style. Freeze burritos in single layer on lightly greased cookie sheet. When fully frozen, wrap burritos individually; place wrapped burritos in large zip-top freezer bags; re-freeze.

To serve: cook in microwave until heated through (about 2 minutes). Or thaw burritos, wrap in foil and bake at 350° for ten minutes.

Additional Ingredient Options:
1 green pepper, finely diced
6 potatoes, shredded and fried until cooked through (or use hashbrowns)
Jalapeno slices
1-2 cloves garlic, finely minced
1 onion, finely diced
1 tomato, peeled and chopped
2 green onions, sliced with tops

MIX-N-MATCH QUICK BREAD
(or Breakfast/Snack Muffins)
Makes two loaves

3 cups flour

1 teaspoon salt

3 teaspoons cinnamon

½ teaspoon baking powder

1 teaspoon baking soda

2 eggs

1 cup oil

2 cups sugar

2 cups MIX-N-MATCH (see below)

3 teaspoons vanilla

1 cup chopped nuts or seeds (your choice)

MIX-N-MATCH (one or more of the following to equal 2 cups):

Apples, grated or chopped

Applesauce

Apricots, chopped

Bananas, mashed or chopped

Berries

Carrots, cooked and mashed or grated

Cherries, pitted and chopped

Coconut, grated

Cranberries, dry or raw, chopped

Dates or figs, pitted and finely chopped

Lemon, ½ cup juice

Marmalade (omit 1 cup sugar)

Mincemeat

Oranges, chopped

Orange juice, ½ cup juice

Peaches, fresh or canned, chopped

Pears, fresh or canned, chopped

Pineapple, crushed and well-drained

Prunes, chopped

Pumpkin, canned

Raisins

Rhubarb, finely chopped (add ½ cup more sugar)

Strawberries, well-drained

Sweet Potato or Yams, cooked and mashed, or grated

Zucchini, grated and well-drained

Directions:

1. Sift together dry ingredients.
2. In separate bowl, beat eggs; add oil and sugar; cream together.
3. Stir in MIX-N-MATCH and vanilla.
4. Add dry ingredients; mix well. Stir in nuts.
5. Spoon into two well-greased loaf pans.
6. Bake at 325° for 1 hour.

Or spoon into muffin tins and bake at 375° for 15 minutes.

When cool, wrap bread in foil; label and freeze. Wrap individual muffins in plastic wrap and then place muffins into large zip-top freezer bag. Muffins can be reheated in microwave. Serve with fresh fruit and juice for a light breakfast.

For tasty Mix-n-Match combinations, try Carrot-Raisin Walnut, or Cranberry-Orange Walnut or Pumpkin-Raisin Sunflower Seed combinations.

LUNCHES

Lunches at home can be prepared easily in advance. Smaller servings of your regular dinner items can be served for a lighter meal. Many items can be frozen and included in brown bag lunches, as well.

Sandwiches:

These freeze well. Fillings that work for freezing include cooked meat, tuna, sliced cheese, cheese spreads, hard cooked egg yolks and nut butters. Use day old bread; spread bread lightly with butter or margarine to prevent fillings soaking into bread; mixing jelly, mayonnaise or salad dressing into the sandwich filling helps prevent soggy bread. Tomatoes and lettuce get limp when frozen, so add these after removing sandwich from freezer. Frozen sandwiches will thaw in lunch boxes in about three to four hours, staying fresh and cooling other foods in the lunch box at the same time.

Quiche:

For lunches, cooked quiche can be frozen in individually wrapped slices. Serve warm (heated in microwave), or cold. Check out the Use-it-Up Quiche, Crustless Quiche, and Crab and Swiss Quiche recipes in this book. See pages 130-135.

Soups:

The following is my favorite recipe for soup—it's simple, creative, delicious and fun! My ten-year-old loves to choose the Mix-n-Match ingredients. This Mix-n-Match Soup recipe is adapted from the book *Cooking Ahead* by Mary Carney.

note: Cooking Ahead by Mary Carney. Used with permission. See
Appendix F for ordering information.

MIX-N-MATCH SOUP
(8-10 servings)

Base or broth ~ Choose one
<u>Tomato</u> ~ one 12-oz. can tomato paste PLUS two 16-oz. cans tomatoes with juice (chopped) *plus* water to equal 10 cups total.
<u>Chicken/Turkey</u> ~ 10 cups broth *or* 4 bouillon cubes dissolved in 10 cups water.
<u>Beef</u> ~ 10 cups broth *or* 4 bouillon cubes dissolved in 10 cups water.

Protein ~ Choose one (1 pound or 2 cups, cooked)
Ground beef, browned
Leftover meatballs or meatloaf, chopped
Cooked chicken or turkey, cut up
Ham, cut up
Dry beans, cooked (pintos, kidney, Great Northern, garbanzos, or a mixture of whatever is on hand)
Lentils (raw)
Frankfurters, sliced (any sausage or Keilbasa)
Pepperoni, sliced

Grain ~ Choose one or two (2 cups)
Rice, cooked (any variety)
Barley, cooked
Pasta, raw
Corn
Dumplings (add at end of cooking time)

Vegetables ~ Choose two or more
(1-2 cups ~ sliced, diced or shredded)
Carrots

Celery

Cabbage

Onion

Potatoes

Tomatoes

Green Beans

Yellow "Wax" Beans

Turnips

Parsnips

Corn

Zucchini

Green Pepper

Peas or pea pods

Cauliflower

Broccoli

Whatever you have around

Seasonings ~ Choose two to four (1-2 teaspoons each)

Basil

Cayenne (dash)

Chives

Cumin

Garlic

Marjoram

Oregano

Parsley

Rosemary

Thyme

Onion powder

To prepare soup:

Bring stock to boil in large stock pot or Dutch oven. Add all ingredients; salt and pepper to taste; reduce heat; simmer one hour.

In crockpot:

Pour boiling stock and other ingredients into crock pot and simmer 8-12 hours or overnight on low setting.

DESSERTS

Many desserts can be prepared ahead and frozen for later use—cakes, pies, cookies, brownies, dessert breads, muffins, cupcakes, etc. I'm only including one actual dessert recipe since most people already have their own family favorites and most dessert items freeze well.

Frequently cake mix boxes go on sale at the grocery store—you can take advantage of the sale prices, stock up on mixes, prepare the cakes in advance, and either freeze them as layers ready to thaw and frost, or cut the cakes into serving sized pieces, wrap individually and use for snacks or desserts in lunch boxes.

Cakes:

Layer, loaf, cupcakes, angel, chiffon, sponge and fruit—prepare as usual, bake and cool. Freeze whole cakes, meal-sized portions or slices. To prevent crushing, freeze whole cakes in boxes. Thaw in wrapping in the refrigerator.

note: for best results, freeze cake and frosting separately, and do not freeze frosting made with egg whites. For ease when frosting frozen cakes, frost frozen cake layers before completely thawed.

Candies:

Fudge, divinity, brittle, taffy and other homemade candies can be frozen. Prepare as usual; wrap each piece individually in plastic wrap; package in rigid freezer containers; freeze.

Cheesecake:

Prepare as usual; bake and cool. Freeze uncovered on cookie sheet. As soon as frozen solid, wrap and re-freeze (place in box or rigid freezer container to prevent crushing).

Cookies:

Baked cookies—prepare as usual; cool; package with freezer paper or waxed paper between layers; label and freeze.

Unbaked cookies—prepare dough as usual; package; label and freeze. Thaw dough in wrapping in the refrigerator. Prepare and bake cookies as usual.

Doughnuts:

Prepare as usual. Cool; package; label and freeze.

note: yeast doughnuts freeze better than cake-type, and glaze soaks into doughnuts when frozen.

Muffins:

Prepare and bake as usual. Cool; package in foil (for reheating in oven) or plastic wrap (for reheating in microwave or eating directly after thawing); place individually wrapped muffins into zip-top freezer bags; label and freeze. Thaw muffins in wrapping to eat cold, or reheat unthawed in foil at 300° for 20 minutes, or reheat unthawed in plastic wrap in microwave for about one minute.

Pies:

When preparing pies for the freezer, pour the unbaked pie filling into lightly greased pie plate; freeze until solid; then pop the frozen pie-shaped filling out of the pie plate and put into a zip-top freezer bag. When it's time to prepare pies, just place the frozen pie-shaped filling into your pie crust; thaw and bake as usual. Easy as... pie!

note: the filling for frozen fruit pies should be a bit thicker than usual.

DEBI'S MILLION DOLLAR CHOCOLATE CHIP COOKIES
(Makes 10 dozen cookies)

I gave a neighbor some of these cookies one day, and he came running back over to my house with an amazed look in his eye. "These are the best chocolate chip cookies I've ever had!" he exclaimed. "You could bake these and market them to local coffee shops!"

2 cups butter

2 cups sugar

2 cups brown sugar

4 eggs

2 teaspoon vanilla

1 teaspoon salt

2 teaspoons baking powder

2 teaspoons soda

4 cups flour

5 cups blended oatmeal *

24 ounces chocolate chips

1 8-ounce chocolate bar (grated)

3 cups chopped walnuts

*First, measure oatmeal. Then blend into a fine powder in a mill or blender.

Directions:

Cream together butter and both sugars. Add eggs and vanilla. Sift together and then stir in salt, baking powder, baking soda and flour. Stir in blended oats. Mix in chips, grated chocolate bar and nuts. Roll into balls, and place two inches apart on cookie sheet. Bake 10 minutes at 375°.

This recipe can be halved, or you can freeze the extras for later.

Recipes for the following dessert items are also included in this book:

Shortcake, see page 166

Snack Cake, see page 167

MULTI-PURPOSE BAKING MIX

This baking mix is similar to the boxed baking mixes you can purchase at the grocery store (i.e. Busquick, Krusteaz, etc.) This particular baking mix recipe contains dry milk already, so you won't be adding more milk when preparing recipes—only water and eggs. Don't use this recipe as a one-to-one substitution for the big name baking mixes, unless you substitute plain water for any added milk in their recipes.

This baking mix can be used in the recipes that follow: pancakes, waffles, biscuits, shortcake, snack cake, dumplings and pizza crust. (All these recipes can be found on the next seven pages.)

4 cups all-purpose flour
4 cups whole wheat flour*
1 1/3 cups nonfat dry milk
¼ cup baking powder
1 teaspoon salt
1½ cups vegetable shortening or margarine (do *not* use oil)

In a large mixing bowl, stir dry ingredients together until well-mixed. Cut in shortening or margarine until well-mixed. Store in closed, covered container. If stored in pantry, use within one month; or store in refrigerator.

note: If margarine is used, store baking mix in refrigerator only—the margarine will go rancid if stored at room temperature for any length of time. Stir lightly before use.

*All-purpose flour, cornmeal or rolled oats can be substituted for the whole wheat flour.

PANCAKES
(Makes about 24 medium-sized pancakes)

4 cups Baking Mix, see page 163
2 cups water
4 eggs, beaten

In a bowl, stir together ingredients just until blended. The mixture will still be somewhat lumpy. Pour scant ¼ cup on to hot griddle. Cook until edges are dry. Turn; cook until golden. For fluffier pancakes: add 4 tablespoons lemon juice (or vinegar), 8 teaspoons sugar and 4 teaspoons baking powder. If preparing pancakes to freeze, undercook slightly, freeze individually on cookie sheet, place frozen pancakes into freezer bag. To reheat, place frozen pancakes in toaster.

WAFFLES
(Makes 24 twelve inch waffles)

4 cups Baking Mix, see page 163
1 1/3 cups water
2 eggs
4 tablespoons vegetable oil

Stir ingredients until blended. Pour on to hot waffle iron. Bake until steaming stops. Freeze leftover waffles individually on cookie sheet. Once frozen, store waffles in a freezer bag. To reheat, place frozen waffles in toaster.

BISCUITS
(Makes 20 two-inch biscuits)

4 cups Baking Mix, see page 163
1 cup water

Add water to Baking Mix and stir about 20 times. Turn dough on to lightly floured board. Knead 10-15 strokes. Roll or pat to ¾ inch thickness and cut with biscuit cutter. Bake on ungreased pan or cookie sheet in a 400° preheated oven for 12-15 minutes. To freeze, place in freezer bag. Reheat in microwave.

Biscuit Variations:
¼ cup bacon, cooked and minced
2/3 cup grated cheese and ½ teaspoon garlic powder
2/3 cup raisins and 2 tablespoons sugar

SHORTCAKE
(12 servings)

4 2/3 cups Baking Mix, see page 163
1 cup water
6 tablespoons sugar
6 tablespoons margarine or butter, melted

Stir ingredients until soft dough forms. Spread in two ungreased 8-inch square baking pans. Bake at 425° for 15-20 minutes or until golden brown. Slice into squares. Serve with sliced berries and whipped cream. For drop shortcake: after stirring, drop dough by ¼ cup drops on to ungreased cookie sheets. Bake 10-12 minutes or until golden brown.

SNACK CAKE
(Makes two 9-inch square cakes)

Topping:
 ½ cup flour
 ¼ cup brown sugar
 ½ teaspoon cinnamon
 2½ tablespoons butter, softened

Cake:
 3 cups Baking Mix, see page 163
 2/3 cup sugar
 1 cup water
 2 eggs
 1 teaspoon vanilla

For topping, combine ingredients with pastry cutter or fork until crumbly; set aside. In large bowl, stir sugar into Baking Mix. In a separate bowl beat water, egg and vanilla until smooth and frothy. Stir egg mixture into Baking Mix; beat until smooth. Pour batter into greased pans; sprinkle with topping. Bake at 350° for 25 minutes, or until firm in the center.

DUMPLINGS

2 cups Baking Mix, see page 163
2/3 cup water

Stir together baking mix and water. Drop by heaping tablespoons on to boiling soup or stew. Cook covered for 10 minutes, then remove lid and cook uncovered for an additional 10 minutes.

PIZZA CRUST
(Makes one 12-inch pizza crust)

This recipe isn't nearly as good as yeast dough, but it'll do in a pinch. It's great if children want to try their hand at making pizza by themselves.

2 cups Baking Mix, see page 163
½ cup water

Stir ingredients together to make soft dough. Knead 6-8 times. Evenly spread out dough on baking sheet; turn up edges slightly. Add toppings (sauce, cheese, meat, vegetables, etc.). Bake at 425° for 20 minutes, or until edges are brown.

10

Money-Saving Tips and Ideas for Groceries

Many people who choose to try freezer-meal cooking do so with the intent of saving money on their grocery bills. Grocery shopping is one of the few semi-flexible expense categories for most families. How much do you spend on groceries? $150 per week? $100? $75? Believe it or not, it's relatively simple to spend as little as $50 per week for a family of five. When I first started investigating frugal food shopping, I was easily spending $600 per month on food and related items at the store. After learning and applying many of the following tips for shopping wisely and planning ahead, I've been able to reduce our family's food bill considerably—often spending as little as $200 per month for groceries (excluding toiletries, cleaning supplies, paper products, etc.).

Probably the greatest help to our family's financial picture has been establishing a budget. Now, don't start hyperventilating and tune me out. I realize the B-word does strange things to people. If the word "budget" makes you sweat and turn purple, try substituting the term "Spending Plan." For some reason, a Spending Plan is psychologically less threatening to many people than a b-b-b-b-b-budget.

The spending plan our family implemented is also known as The Envelope System. It's easy, relatively painless and it works. This simple plan did more to turn around our financial picture than any other single change we've made in our spending habits.

First, we figured out how much money we needed each month for the different expense categories (food, clothing, gasoline, bus fare, coffee at work, etc.), and placed that amount of cash (yes, the green paper stuff!) into separately labeled envelopes. We then had a concrete visual aid to show us exactly how much money we had left to spend in each category. And we clearly saw how borrowing money from one envelope left us less money in another. And once the money's gone, it's gone.

The Envelope System is perfect for people who tend to think if there's a positive balance in the checkbook, they can keep writing checks. Shopping with cash in hand also tends to make people more aware of the reality of the money they're spending. It feels more "real" to part with a handful of ten dollar bills than just writing out a check for the same eighty-dollars.

My husband and I learned this simple budgeting trick from the old Marlo Thomas television show, "That Girl." In our case, life imitated art. (Maybe claiming That Girl, as "art" is stretching the analogy a bit too far.)

There's no magic formula to living within your means, whatever those means might be. I've known people living beneath the poverty line who never go into debt and never have outstanding bills. I've also seen families living in the grandest homes in town struggling to stay afloat each month due to overspending. Whether you're a financially strapped one income family, a single working mother or father, or a double income family with mounting consumer debt, we can all use a good dose of reality in the financial area of our lives.

The following one hundred easy tips should help you gain some control over your grocery bills and food-related spending.

GENERAL MONEY SAVING FOOD TIPS

1) Go grocery shopping with cash only. Leave your credit cards, debit cards and checkbook at home. Keep a running total of the groceries in your cart as you shop. If you overspend your grocery budget, you'll need to put something back on the shelf or re-shop for less expensive alternatives.

2) Avoid prepackaged items and convenience foods. Homemade alternatives are almost always cheaper.

3) Think of meat as a side dish or condiment and serve in smaller portions.

4) Eat meat less frequently.

5) If your ideology allows, make friends with a hunter or fisherman who is willing to share their bounty.

6) At mealtimes serve everyone a single glass of juice or milk. Make refills plain water.

7) If you really need to keep food costs down, drink water only. Be sure your children are getting adequate servings of dairy products in other forms if you don't serve milk as a beverage.

8) Make your own seasoning mixes.

9) Make dessert a special treat rather than an every night occurrence.

10) Bake cakes from scratch—much cheaper and often as easy as using a packaged mix or purchasing prepared cakes from the bakery.

11) Popcorn is one of the least expensive snacks you'll find.

12) Buy large bags of pretzels, chips and other snack items on sale. Re-package them into small zip-top bags to pop into lunches.

13) Learn to cook beans.

14) Make your own bread crumbs and croutons from leftover bread and crusts.

15) Use powdered milk that you've reconstituted in baked goods and any recipes that call for milk (soups, sauces, etc.).

16) Butter and margarine wrappers can be used to grease baking pans and foil. Store your butter wrappers in a large zip-top bag in the freezer, pulling one out when needed.

17) On Sundays make a regular breakfast, serve your main meal in the afternoon after church, and then use up the week's leftovers for a light evening meal.

18) For homegrown fruit, raspberries are easy to raise and they can make a nice hedge at the edge of your yard. Rather than planting ornamental shade trees, plant fruit trees (apple, pear, cherry, etc.).

19) If you don't have room for a garden in your yard, try growing salad vegetables in containers on your porch or deck.

20) Herbs can be grown indoors in small pots near a bright window.

21) When you have a baby, consider breastfeeding. Mother's milk is healthy and free, and free is the best price of all!

22) Make your own baby food. Family food can be quickly chopped or blended in a food processor or blender. Scoop homemade baby foods into ice cube trays and freeze. Pop out the frozen food cubes and place into large freezer bags. When it's time to feed baby, take out the amount of cubes you'll need; heat and serve.

23) When entertaining at home, invite people over for an evening of light snacks and desserts. If you must serve dinner, make it potluck. You can provide the main dish, drinks, plates and silverware, while each guest brings a salad, dessert or side dish.

24) When dining out, go at lunch time or breakfast rather than dinner. Luncheon menus are often half the price of dinner menus but many times offer the same general selection of items.

25) To save further when dining out, order only water to drink. Ask for a lemon or lime wedge to make it special.

26) Find out if there's a SHARE program in your area. SHARE is a food buying co-op where you get a box or bag full of food valued at $35-$40 for only $14 plus two hours community service. (The community service can even be something like working in a church nursery, volunteering for the PTA, helping a shut-in neighbor or teaching Sunday School.)

SAVING STRATEGIES FOR GROCERY SHOPPING

27) Set your grocery budget and then make up your menus and shopping list to fit your budget, rather than the other way around.

28) One simple approach to meal planning is to set price goals for each meal. For example: Breakfast price goal = $0.50 per person per meal; Dinner price goal = $3-$4 per meal total. If you know you can make a home cooked meal for only $4, it will be less tempting to make a quick (and expensive!) trip to the local drive-thru window.

29) Prepare a Master Shopping List of items you buy regularly. Add additional items as needed.

30) Always check store flyers for their weekly specials and private coupons.

31) No impulse buying, ever! Stick to your shopping list religiously.

32) Take a calculator with you to the grocery store for comparing unit prices and to keep a running total of purchases.

33) Keep a list of sale prices of various foods you buy regularly. When you see something on sale you can check your price list to see if it's really a good buy, or not. If it is, stock up. It's so important to know your prices. Just because an item is advertised as a "sale item" it doesn't mean it's necessarily a good buy.

34) Don't buy non-food items at the grocery store. These items (housewares, greeting cards, over-the-counter medicines, toiletries, etc.) can be purchased elsewhere for less money.

35) Don't shop when you're hungry. You're more likely to make impulse buys when your stomach is grumbling.

36) Try not to shop with children. "Helpers" tend to add more items to your grocery cart while also distracting you from the task at hand.

37) Take your time shopping. It pays to examine labels, check cost per serving, compare brands, etc.

38) Be sure to look on the lowest and highest shelves for bargains. Stores often place the highest-priced items at eye level.

39) Never buy an item stacked at the end of an aisle unless you're certain it's on sale. Often stores will display their sale items with expensive non-sale items. For example, spaghetti sauce may be on sale, but then displayed with the discounted sauce could be the store's most expensive brand of pasta and Parmesan cheese.

40) Check to see if your local grocery store offers any Preferred Shopper programs for loyal shoppers.

41) Shop at a local farmer's market.

42) Use coupons for items and brands you normally buy.

43) Always check the expiration date on your coupons.

44) If you give the cashier your coupons up front, you'll be less likely to forget about the coupons later on. Or carry your coupons in an envelope along with your shopping list.

45) Whenever possible, buy in bulk (but check unit pricing to make sure you're really getting a bargain).

46) Join a warehouse shopping club for your bulk purchases, but once again, remember to keep track of unit pricing. This is a time when keeping a price list of items you frequently buy can really pay off. You'll be amazed how many times items at the warehouse store aren't really cheaper per pound than the sale prices at the supermarket.

47) Buying in bulk frequently? Contact the manufacturer directly and save even more money.

48) Watch closely as the cashier rings up your groceries with an electronic scanner. Occasionally the scanner will come up with an incorrect price. Some stores will give you incorrectly scanned items for free!

49) Ask the store manager if you can browse through their dented can collection—usually sold for pennies on the dollar. Stores often sell diapers and other products for a discount if the bags have been ripped or opened.

50) Check store entrances for special flyers and don't forget to look in local newspapers for additional coupons.

51) Get a rain check if an advertised item is out of stock.

52) If anything you buy is spoiled, return it.

53) Paper products can run up your "food" bill. Use cloth kitchen towels and napkins, laundering them frequently.

FOOD PURCHASING SPECIFICS

54) Give store brands a try. The prices are often 20-50% below similar name brand products. You won't know which store brands are good unless you're willing to take a chance and try them. If you find a tasty, high quality store brand or generic product, you'll save money. But still remember to compare prices. The sale price of a brand name product will sometimes be lower than the regular price of a store brand.

55) Boneless and skinless chicken is very expensive. Buy whole birds if you really want to save money (use the bones for soup to stretch your purchase further).

56) Check with local farmers to see if anyone is selling beef. You can often purchase half a beef for less than one-dollar per pound (which includes steaks, roasts, etc.—not just ground beef).

57) When purchasing basic grocery supplies (rice, beans, pasta, flour, oatmeal, vegetable oil, tuna, etc.) buy for the lowest cost available with the least amount of packaging.

58) Buy spices in bulk.

59) Buy cheese in large quantities when it goes on sale. Grate the cheese and freeze in zip-top freezer bags. To use, just take out the amount of cheese you need and keep the rest frozen.

60) Purchase plain frozen vegetables and make your own seasonings and sauce rather than buying the expensive frozen vegetables in ready-made sauce.

61) Large bags of fresh potatoes are usually a good buy. Store in a cool, dark place.

62) Buy produce in-season and on sale.

63) Watch for sales on bulk ground meats. Divide the meat into one pound batches and freeze in individual freezer bags.

64) Find out when your store's meat department marks down meats. If the store is running a sale on ground beef for $0.88 per pound, and then they mark down their meat half price on a particular day, you may be able to purchase packages for as little as $0.33 per pound.

65) Bakery, dairy and produce departments often mark down items for quick sale. Ask the department managers what time of day they usually do this.

66) Buy large quantities of bread, rolls and other baked goods at bakery outlet stores and freeze the bread items. You can often find top-quality multi-grain breads for as little as four loaves for one-dollar. The usual outlet price in my area is around $0.50 per loaf for name brand multi-grain breads. Compare that to paying $2-$3 for the very same bread in the supermarket.

67) Buy grains, flours, sugars and dry beans from a grocery warehouse or food co-op.

68) When purchasing pre-bagged produce (apples, oranges, potatoes, etc.), weigh several bags to find the heaviest one. A five pound bag of apples has a minimum of five pounds, but could actually contain a pound or two more. This will lower your price per pound.

BREAKFAST IDEAS

69) Serve oatmeal as your regular breakfast meal (not the instant kind). If you buy in bulk or use store brands, you usually can't find a less expensive breakfast. Dress oatmeal up with raisins, brown sugar, cinnamon, jam, bits of fruit or whatever makes it special for your family.

70) Other inexpensive breakfast ideas: muffins, pancakes, waffles, French toast, Cream of Wheat, homemade egg sandwiches.

71) For inexpensive syrups, use store brands or homemade.

72) On Saturdays serve a late morning brunch. Make a big batch of pancakes or other economical breakfast meal, allowing extras for afternoon snacking.

73) Large boxes of breakfast cereal are often much cheaper per serving than small convenience sizes. The least expensive form of cereal to purchase is usually packaged in plastic bags rather than cardboard boxes.

74) Buy juices as frozen concentrate—saving about half the cost of bottled juice.

75) Serve breakfast juice in small juice glasses rather than larger beverage glasses. It really makes the juice stretch.

76) Learn to make omelets. They're economical; a good source of protein; and a great way to use up leftover meats, vegetables and cheeses.

77) Rice (brown or converted), barley, and other whole grains can be cooked and eaten just like oatmeal.

LUNCH TIPS

78) Use leftovers to make homemade frozen TV dinners that you can take to work and warm in the microwave.

79) Most people spend at least $5 per workday on food-related items at work (lunch, pop, coffee, snacks, etc.). Bringing lunches, snacks, sodas, and a thermos of coffee from home can easily save $100 per month—or $1,200 per year!

80) Pack lunches for your kids to take to school, rather than purchasing school lunches.

81) Sandwiches made from the old standby, peanut butter and jelly, are still a hit with kids today.

82) Lunch meat is usually cheaper per pound if purchased at the deli counter rather than prepackaged containers.

83) Pack reusable thermos bottles filled with juice or milk instead of buying individual disposable juice boxes.

84) Pack your own gelatin, pudding, applesauce and fruit cup snacks for school lunches in small, plastic, reusable containers.

85) Purchase lunch box snacks and desserts at the bakery thrift store and freeze.

86) For dessert, pack a slice of homemade cake or a brownie. These treats can be baked ahead of time, sliced into serving sizes and then frozen. The frozen treats can go directly into the lunch box and will be defrosted by noon.

87) Keep lunches at home simple: sandwiches, soups, salads, fresh fruit, sliced cheese, crackers.

88) Make your own homemade soups from leftovers for lunch. You can also pack the soup in thermos containers for lunches away from home.

DINNER MEAL STRETCHERS

89) Stretch each whole chicken purchase into three meals (I've heard this idea referred to as "Rubber Chicken"—you just keep stretching it out!). Use the joint pieces for a meal of barbecued, fried or baked chicken. Cut up the breast meat and use in a casserole or skillet meal. Save the bones and any leftover meat for homemade chicken soup.

90) In some parts of the country, ground turkey is less expensive than other ground meats. If this is the case in your area, substitute ground turkey in your ground beef recipes.

91) Substitute turkey ham and turkey sausages in recipes.

92) Keep ingredients on hand for several quick and easy meals. When time is scarce you won't be as tempted to run out to the local drive-thru for a fast meal. Freezer-meals help with this, too.

93) Occasionally serve breakfast for dinner. Even when prepared in a big way, breakfast is one of the most economical meals to make. At our house we rarely have time for a big breakfast of pancakes, eggs, bacon and fruit in the morning, so it's a special treat to have a meal like that for dinner.

94) Omelets are fun and economical dinner meals, too. You can serve them with almost any side dishes (not just breakfast-type items).

95) Stretch your meat by adding oatmeal or dry bread crumbs to ground meat. Flavor the meat with herbs.

96) Vegetable and noodle casseroles with meat are good budget stretchers.

97) Turkey is usually a better value per pound than chicken. Substitute cooked turkey in your cooked chicken recipes, and use leftover turkey for sandwiches and casseroles.

98) Larger turkeys have a higher proportion of meat to bone, making them more economical.

99) Save electricity or gas by cooking several items in the oven at one time.

100) Cook up a big pot of soup for dinner one night during the weekend, and you'll be set with several easy lunches for the week.

APPENDIX A

FOODS THAT DON'T FREEZE WELL

1) Mayonnaise separates. It can be used in limited amounts if mixed with other ingredients in a sauce or casserole.

2) Sour cream becomes watery, but can also be used same ways as mayonnaise.

3) Fried foods lose crispness and become soggy.

4) Soft cheese (cream cheese) often becomes watery, so don't use alone. It can be used mixed into recipes, however.

5) Potatoes cooked in soups and stews can become mushy and dark. Save potatoes to add raw just before freezing, making sure to cover them completely with soup or stew liquid.

6) Cake icings made with egg whites, cream fillings, soft frostings and custard or cream filled pies don't freeze well.

7) Cooked egg whites become tough and rubbery.

FOODS THAT CHANGE IN THE FREEZER

1) Raw vegetables lose crispness, but can be cooked or used for soups, stews and casserole-type recipes.

2) Gravies and fat-based sauces may separate and will need to be recombined after thawing. Stir during reheating to recombine.

3) Thickened sauces may need to be thinned after freezing; stir in a small amount of milk or broth.

4) Some seasonings can change flavor during freezing (i.e. onion, garlic, black pepper, cloves, cinnamon, nutmeg, vanilla, almond and mint extracts, thyme, rosemary, basil, dill, sage). For best flavor, add herbs and other seasonings when meal is reheated.

5) Heavy cream can be frozen, but won't whip.

6) Milk can be frozen for drinking, but will often separate and need to be shaken or stirred to recombine.

7) Vegetables, pastas and grains are softer following freezing and reheating. Undercook before freezing. If you're adding noodles to soups, either add the raw noodles after thawing so they will cook during the reheating process, or add raw noodles to the soup after cooling and just before freezing.

8) Cheeses often change texture in the freezer. Many hard cheeses become crumbly—use in recipes but not for slicing. Hard cheeses freeze best if grated before freezing.

APPENDIX B

RECIPE EQUIVALENTS

Recipes will often call for two cups diced onions or three cups grated cheese. This makes it difficult to know how many whole onions to buy or what quantity of block cheese to add to your shopping list. The following equivalents for common recipe ingredients are approximate:

1 medium onion = 1 cup, diced

1 medium green pepper = 1 cup, diced

3 ounces fresh mushrooms = 1 cup, sliced

2 large celery ribs = 1 cup, sliced or diced

2 cups margarine or butter = 1 pound

1 medium clove garlic = 1 teaspoon, minced

1 medium apple = 1 cup, chopped

4-5 cups noodles = 8 ounces uncooked

8 ounces uncooked spaghetti = 4 cups cooked

1 pound ground beef = 2 ½ cups browned

1 medium tomato = 1 cup chopped

1 pound flour - 3 ½ cups

8 slices bacon = ½ cup crumbled

4 ounces (¼ pound) cheese = 1 cup, grated

1 pound ham = 3 cups, cubed

3-4 pound whole chicken = 4 cups cooked meat

EQUIVALENT MEASURES

1 tablespoon = 3 teaspoons, ½ fluid ounce

2 tablespoons = 1 fluid ounce

4 tablespoons = ¼ cup

8 tablespoons = ½ cup

16 tablespoons = 1 cup

Equivalent Measures

1 cup = ½ pint, 8 fluid ounces

2 cups = 1 pint

4 cups = 1 quart

4 quarts = 1 liquid gallon

APPENDIX C

TIPS FOR SINGLES

1) Whenever you cook a meal with more than one serving, freeze the extras in individual serving sizes. Most foods can be frozen in single servings and reheated in the microwave.

2) Freeze individual portions of baked chicken, quiche, pizza, etc., in sandwich bags. Then pack the bagged portions into one large freezer bag, label, date and freeze. If you have company, just pull out the number of individual servings you'll need from the bag and reheat.

3) Prepare things in advance that can be used in more than one way: meatballs, stew, chili, spaghetti sauce, etc.

4) Save time and effort by cooking similar recipes at once. If you purchase a whole chicken, you can make several meals from that one purchase: chicken soup, baked chicken, chicken tacos, etc.

5) Restaurant supply stores often carry individual aluminum foil containers or freezer-to-microwave pans.

6) Try a cooperative effort. Find a single friend (or two!) to cook with and divide the frozen meals between you.

APPENDIX D

REDUCING FAT IN RECIPES

1) For sour cream, substitute non-fat sour cream or non-fat plain yogurt.

2) For cream cheese, substitute an equal amount of yogurt cheese. To make yogurt cheese, place plain yogurt into the center of a piece of cheese cloth or a coffee filter, and let the liquid (whey) drain out into a bowl. You can save the whey to use in making soup stock or to replace liquid in bread and other recipes.

3) Cream soups are high in fat. If creaminess is needed, use non-fat evaporated milk—a perfect substitute for cream in recipes. Mix non-fat evaporated milk with lightly cooked mushrooms, celery, or chicken (with broth) to make your own flavored cream soups. Instead of Cream-of-Whatever soup, you can also double or triple the amount of vegetables called for in the recipe and then puree half the vegetables in a blender or food processor.

4) If a recipe requires you to sauté vegetables in butter, margarine or oil, place the chopped vegetables into a covered and vented microwave-safe bowl with a small amount of water or vegetable broth. Microwave on high until softened.

5) Using non-stick cookware cuts down dramatically on the amount of fat and oils used in cooking.

6) Use the strongest flavor cheese you can buy and then use half the recommended amount. If a recipe calls for one cup medium cheddar, try one-half cup sharp cheddar instead.

7) Instead of chicken or beef stock, use homemade vegetable stock. Save all the peelings and end pieces from vegetables. Keep a container or bag in the refrigerator or freezer just for peelings. When the container's full, place the peelings into a crockpot or large stock pot along with some sliced onion, celery, carrots, garlic, herbs, etc., and cook on low-heat all day. Strain out the vegetables and you'll have a tasty, healthy vegetable stock.

8) To de-fat chicken stock after boiling chicken, let the stock cool, then refrigerate it for several hours. The fat will rise to the surface and solidify so you can easily skim it off with a spoon.

9) After frying ground beef, drain thoroughly in a colander and then rinse well with hot water.

10) Rather than frying ground beef, try boiling it. Bring a large stock pot full of water to a boil. Place raw ground beef into boiling water, stirring to separate. Boil until meat is cooked through. Drain. You can save the water you boiled the meat in, place the container of broth in the refrigerator; let the fat rise; skim off the fat and use the ground beef cooking water in soup.

11) In sweet baked goods, an equal amount of applesauce or prune puree can be used instead of oil.

APPENDIX E

CREATIVE USES FOR FREEZER MEALS

Freezer Meal Baby Shower

I believe one of the greatest gifts for a new mom is a freezer full of homecooked food—especially for a mother with older children at home, too. This type of Baby Shower works best if hosted before the baby's arrival, rather than after. Have each guest bring one or two favorite frozen meals to send home with the mom-to-be. You can also include frozen side-dishes and desserts.

Meals for Others

Many individuals and churches provide homecooked meals for the sick, new moms, families in crisis, etc. I've found by having a handy supply of freezer meals, I can easily provide a meal for someone who's going through a difficult time. Often I will purposely prepare a couple of extra meals each month for giving to others. A church I attended when my first baby was born had a ministry called Moms Helping Moms. One of the main aspects of the Moms ministry was to provide meals for the new moms in the church. The freezer full of food I received after giving birth to a premature baby was one of the greatest things ever done for me.

Cooking with a Friend

Many freezer meal cooks find that cooking with a partner can be a lot of fun. Some things you need to take into consideration when choosing a cooking partner are: family size, how well you get along, basic tastes in food and special diets. You can also benefit by sharing cookware, appliances and knowledge. Try to get together in person to do your planning session. Share a dozen of your respective families' favorite tried-and-true recipes. Try to find 10 recipes you can both agree on, preparing three meals of each recipe for a month's worth of food. Go through the regular Frozen Assets planning and preparation steps together. It helps if you divide the various duties beforehand—maybe one of you can do the shopping one month while the other takes care of baby-sitting duties; and someone could prepare chicken meals while the other prepares ground beef meals. Be sure to label the frozen meals with each person's name as you're preparing the meals for freezing. One potential difficulty of cooking with someone else is lack of freezer space during cooking day. You might want to plan on cooking at the home of whoever has the most available freezer space. Also, have several picnic coolers handy for transporting frozen meals to your home.

Group Meal Exchange

If you know a group of people interested or experienced in cooking for the freezer, you can arrange a group meal exchange. This is sometimes referred to as a freezer potluck. If you have 10 people in your group, everyone would prepare 10 family-sized portions of one recipe. Then the group would get together every ten days to exchange meals. A meal exchange works best if done with similar sized families with similar tastes. Each member of the group could also prepare 30 family-sized portions of a single recipe and then exchange meals only once a month (eating the same meal three times during the month). To discover meals that most people in the group would like, ask each group member what their three family favorite meals are, or what they frequently serve to company. This potluck technique works well for the people I know who have tried it—each family gets a variety of frozen meals without one person having to do all the cooking.

This method of cooking for the freezer would also be helpful for groups of singles. Singles would only need to prepare 30 single-serving meals.

Organizing a frozen meal exchange for members of a local senior center would be a great way to ensure that single seniors are eating properly.

APPENDIX F

RECOMMENDED RESOURCES

FREEZER MEAL BOOKS

Cooking Ahead, by Mary Carney

As a homeschooling mother of four, minister's wife, frequent seminar speaker and freelance writer, Mary Carney has depended on her *Cooking Ahead* techniques to simplify her busy life. For ordering information, write to: Mary Carney, c/o Simple Living Workshops, P.O. Box 174, Advance, Indiana 46102.

Once-a-Month Cooking, by Mimi Wilson and Mary Beth Lagerborg

This book revolutionized the way I feed my family. Although I found the recipes too expensive for my limited grocery budget, I discovered by applying their methods to my own recipes I've saved substantial time, energy and money each month. (ISBN: 1561792462)

Dinner's in the Freezer, by Jill Bond
(ISBN: 0964539608, $20.00)

30 Day Gourmet, by Nanci Slagle and Tara Wohlenhaus

Colorful three-ring binder with recipes arranged according to main protein group. 30 Day Gourmet emphasizes sharing your big cooking day with a friend, containing charts and planning sheets to simplify cooking with someone else. This manual must be purchased directly from the authors. $25 + $5 shipping and handling. Write to: 30 Day Gourmet, P.O. Box 272, Brownsburg, Indiana 46112.

COOKING-RELATED BOOKS

Cheapskate in the Kitchen, by Mary Hunt

Learn to prepare delicious gourmet meals for a fraction of the cost of restaurant dining. (I contributed several recipes to this book.) (ISBN: 0312961073, $4.99)

Eat Healthy for $50 a Week, by Rhonda Barfield

Feed your family nutritious delicious meals for less. Yes, it really is possible to feed your family healthy meals for $50 per week. Barfield shows you how. (ISBN: 1575660180, $12.00)

Mix-n-Match Recipes, by Deborah Taylor-Hough

Simple and creative recipes using common ingredients—a great way to use up leftovers. Soup, quiche, skillet meals, casseroles, dessert breads, and more. Send $5 to: Simple Pleasures Press, P.O. Box 941, Auburn, Washington 98071-0941. Be sure to specify *Mix-n-Match Recipes* when ordering.

More-With-Less Cookbook, by Doris Longacre

The classic, thoughtful cookbook published by the Mennonites—every kitchen needs this book on the shelf. (ISBN: 0836117867)

FRUGAL LIVING

Many people choose freezer meal methods for the money-saving advantages. Here are some more resource down the frugal living path.

Simple Living, by Deborah Taylor-Hough

A collection of helpful money-saving tips, ideas and resources. Putting just one of these ideas to action could easily save you the cost of this booklet. Send $5 to: Simple Pleasures Press, P.O. Box 941, Auburn, Washington 98071-0941. Specify *Simple Living* when ordering.

Miserly Moms, by Jonni McCoy

Practical book for living well on a limited budget. McCoy shares her "Eleven Miserly Guidelines" that will help you trim expenses on everything from groceries to household cleaners. Lots of helpful recipes and tips. Includes a chapter on bulk cooking. (ISBN: 1888306149, $9.99)

ON-LINE RESOURCES
Frozen Assets Web Pages

http://members.aol.com/OAMCLoop/index.html

Dedicated to freezer meal cooking techniques. Recipes, tips, Message Board, many helpful freezer-related links. A must see! Updated regularly.

Simple/Frugal Living

http://members.aol.com/DSimple/index.html

Tips, quotes, articles, Message Board, lots of links. Updated weekly.

Frugal Books for Simple Living

http://members.aol.com/DSimple/books.html

Small on-line bookstore of frugal and simple living books. Many of the books listed in this Appendix can be ordered on-line from this web-page. (Operated in association with Amazon.com.)

Busy Cooks

http://busycooks.miningco.com/

Regular features on freezer meals, planned leftovers, quick cooking recipes, easy entertaining and more.

FROZEN ASSETS

Monthly Menu Planner

FROZEN ASSETS

Monday	Tuesday	Wednesday	Thursday	Friday	Saturday	Sunday

Recipes

Name of dish _____ Servings _____

NOTES:

Ingredients:

_____

_____

_____

_____

_____

_____

_____

Preparation Instructions:

_____

_____

_____

_____

_____

Freezing Instructions:

_____

_____

Thawing and Cooking Instructions:

_____

_____

Recipes

Name of dish _____ Servings _____

NOTES:	Ingredients:

Ingredients:

_____

_____

_____

_____

_____

_____

_____

Preparation Instructions:

_____

_____

_____

_____

_____

Freezing Instructions:

_____

_____

Thawing and Cooking Instructions:

_____

_____

Recipes

Name of dish _____ Servings _____

NOTES:

Ingredients:

_____
_____
_____
_____
_____
_____
_____

Preparation Instructions:

_____
_____
_____
_____
_____

Freezing Instructions:

_____
_____

Thawing and Cooking Instructions:

_____
_____

Recipes

Name of dish _____ Servings _____

NOTES:

Ingredients:

_____
_____
_____
_____
_____
_____
_____

Preparation Instructions:

_____
_____
_____
_____
_____

Freezing Instructions:

_____
_____

Thawing and Cooking Instructions:

_____
_____

Recipes

Name of dish _____ Servings _____

NOTES:

Ingredients:

_____

_____

_____

_____

_____

_____

_____

Preparation Instructions:

_____

_____

_____

_____

_____

Freezing Instructions:

_____

_____

Thawing and Cooking Instructions:

_____

_____

Recipes

Name of dish _____ Servings _____

NOTES:

Ingredients:

_____

_____

_____

_____

_____

_____

_____

Preparation Instructions:

_____

_____

_____

_____

_____

Freezing Instructions:

_____

_____

Thawing and Cooking Instructions:

_____

_____

Recipes

Name of dish _____ Servings _____

NOTES:

Ingredients:

_____
_____
_____
_____
_____
_____
_____

Preparation Instructions:

_____
_____
_____
_____
_____

Freezing Instructions:

_____
_____

Thawing and Cooking Instructions:

_____
_____

FROZEN

- ☐ _____
- ☐ _____
- ☐ _____
- ☐ _____
- ☐ _____
- ☐ _____
- ☐ _____
- ☐ _____
- ☐ _____
- ☐ _____

STAPLES

- ☐ _____
- ☐ _____
- ☐ _____
- ☐ _____
- ☐ _____
- ☐ _____
- ☐ _____
- ☐ _____

FREEZING SUPPLIES

- ☐ _____
- ☐ _____
- ☐ _____
- ☐ _____
- ☐ _____
- ☐ _____
- ☐ _____
- ☐ _____

FREEZER BAGS, FOILS ALUMINUM TRAYS

- ☐ _____
- ☐ _____
- ☐ _____
- ☐ _____
- ☐ _____
- ☐ _____
- ☐ _____
- ☐ _____
- ☐ _____
- ☐ _____
- ☐ _____

MISC.

- ☐ _____
- ☐ _____
- ☐ _____
- ☐ _____
- ☐ _____
- ☐ _____
- ☐ _____
- ☐ _____
- ☐ _____
- ☐ _____
- ☐ _____
- ☐ _____
- ☐ _____
- ☐ _____
- ☐ _____

RECIPE INDEX
by Main Ingredient

ALSO FROM
CHAMPION PRESS, LTD.

365 Quick, Easy and
Inexpensive Dinner Menus
by Penny E. Stone
ISBN 1-891400-33-9
$19.95

365 Quick, Easy and Inexpensive Dinner Menus meets all the needs of every home cook. This new release tastefully combines nutrition, ease of preparation and cost-efficiency while offering not just single dish recipes but full meal *menus—one for every day of the year*! With homespun charm, warm wit and playful trivia, home-cooks are provided with a ready-made plan for entire meals that are fun, cheap and quick. *365 Quick, Easy and Inexpensive Dinner Menus* is a cookbook for the entire family and its innovative menus have been approved by kids nationwide. The book is multi-indexed: by food category and by preparation time.

Also by Deborah Taylor-Hough...

A Simple Choice: a practical guide for saving your time, money and sanity
$14.95
ISBN 1-891400-49-5

The number one complaint of people today is the lack of meaning in their hectic lives. In her second book, *A Simple Choice: A practical guide for saving your time, money and sanity*, author Deborah Taylor-Hough addresses societal emptiness and personal search for purpose. With an aim toward returning readers to emotional replenishment using clear, concise and uplifting examples, *A Simple Choice* not only examines the futility of keeping up with the Jones's but depicts the simply joy and fulfillment of keeping up with ourselves. In an era of self-reflection *A Simple Choice* holds the mirror of life's simple joys that are available to everyone.

THE SINGLE PARENT RESOURCE

FINALLY! THE PROVEN ANSWERS SINGLE PARENTS NEED

by Brook Noel with Art Klein
ISBN: 1-891400-44-4 $13.95

What kind of help do single parents need most in their day-to-day lives? The authors asked that question to over 500 single parents. Now they provide the answers to the top concerns, problems and challenges of single-parent life. Here they are—practical, concise, timely, relevant—and never before available in a single guide!

TO ORDER CALL (360) 576 9261
or visit our web site at www.championpress.com

A Charlotte Mason Education

by Catherine Levison
ISBN 1-891400-16-9 $8.95

The immensely popular ideas of Charlotte Mason have inspired educators for many decades. Her unique methodology as written about in her six-volume series established the necessary protocols for an education above and beyond that which can be found in traditional classroom settings. *In A Charlotte Mason Education*, Catherine Levison has collected the key points of Charlotte Mason's methods and presents them in a simple, straightforward way that will allow families to quickly maximize the opportunities of home schooling. With weekly schedules, a challenging and diverse curriculum will both inspire and educate your child. *A Charlotte Mason Education* is the latest tool for parents seeking the best education for their children.

More Charlotte Mason Education

by Catherine Levison
ISBN 1-891400-17-7 $13.95

Thousands of home educators benefited from the practical ideas contained in Catherine Levison's primer, *A Charlotte Mason Education*. Now Catherine takes an in-depth journey offering even more ideas for implementing the popular methods of Charlotte Mason into home schooling. In this concise and practical guide, Levison presents the key points of Charlotte Mason's methods as contained in her six-volume series. A perfect companion to her first book, *More Charlotte Mason Education* will continue to guide your family down an enjoyable and successful path of home schooling

TO ORDER CALL (360) 576 9261
or visit our web site at www.championpress.com

Back to Basics

101 Ideas for Stengthening our Children and our Families
by Brook Noel
ISBN: 1-891400-48-7 $13.95

"Life is what happens while we're making other plans," the adage goes, but how far have modern families let that attitude take root? Too far, it would seem, when a recent survey found that the average working mother spends 50 minutes a day with her child. The average working father? Nine! It doesn't have to be. In her new book, author Brook Noel confronts the issues that continue to tear at the modern social fabric. Noel's collection of insights offers a much-needed road map back to the values that are the foundation for strong homes and strong families.

I Wasn't Ready to Say Goodbye:
surviving, coping and healing
after the sudden death of a loved one
by Brook Noel and Pamela D. Blair, Ph.D.
ISBN 1-891400-27-4 $14.95

Each year about eight million Americans suffer the death of a close family member. The list of high visibility disasters, human suffering and sudden loss is long and will continue to grow. From TWA Flight 800 to Egypt Air, from Oklahoma City to Columbine, daily we face incomprehensible loss. Outside the publicized tragedies there are many families and individuals that are suffering behind closed doors in our neighborhoods, in our own homes, in hospital waiting rooms. Now for those who face the challenges of sudden death, there is a hand to hold written by two women who have experienced sudden loss. In a book that will touch, comfort, uplift and console, the authors explore sudden death and its role in the cycle of life.

EDUCATIONAL AND GROUP DISCOUNTS ARE AVAILABLE FOR MORE
INFORMATION WRITE TO CHAMPION PRESS, LTD.

Please photocopy this page to order additional copies of *Frozen Assets*. Or on-line at our web site, www.championpress.com.

QUANTITY

_____ *Frozen Assets* by Deborah Taylor-Hough $14.95

_____ Shipping and handling. $2.95 for the first book and $1 more for each additional book

_____ Payment enclosed
_____ Please charge my ___ Visa ___ MasterCard

Account Number _____

Expiration Date _____

Signature _____

Name as it appears on card _____

Name _____

Address _____

City _____ State _____ Zip _____

Day Phone _____

Champion Press, Ltd.
500 W Bradley Road A129
Fox Point WI 53217
www.championpress.com

Enjoy all the time and money-saving benefits of the once-a-month-cooking method... while losing weight at the same time!

You asked for it--and you got it. Deborah Taylor-Hough has created 20+ one-week menus that you can mix and match to create an abundant supply of healthy, easy, freezer meals!

ISBN 1-891400-19-3 Price: $19.95

Healthy Foods:
an irreverent guide to understanding nutrition and feeding your family well
by Leanne Ely, C.N.C.

Plagued by picky eaters? Thinking "Health Food" equals "Granola Food?" Do you consider ketchup a vegetable in your child's diet? Help is here. With a humorous touch, Leanne will show you how to make nutrition a priority in your family--without battles at the table. Includes many child and parent-friendly recipes.

ISBN 1-891400-20-7 $19.95